Work Smarter, Not Harder

Experts Reveal Insights & Techniques that Can Help You Experience More Accomplishment, Satisfaction, Energy, and Delight — at Both Work & Home

Compiled by Doug Smart

James & Brookfield
J&B
Publishers

Work Smarter, Not Harder

Managing Editor: Gayle Smart

Editor: Sara Kahan
Proofreader: Rose Taylor
Book Designer: Paula Chance

Disclaimer: This book is a compilation of ideas from numerous experts who have each contributed a chapter. As such, the views expressed in each chapter are those of the authors and not necessarily the views of James & Brookfield Publishers.

For more information, contact:
James & Brookfield Publishers
P.O. Box 768024
Roswell, GA 30076
✆ 770-587-9784

Library of Congress Catalog Number in Publication Data

ISBN: 0-9749191-0-1

10 9 8 7 6 5 4 3 2 1

TABLE OF CONTENTS

Stay the Driver . . . not the Driven

by Michelle M. Weil, Ph.D.

Today we are driven personally, professionally, and as a society. ***Driven***. No doubt about it. For example, even though most of us know we need to take time to breathe, if you ask someone to breathe, he jokingly or unknowingly hyperventilates! We live in a world greatly overrun by our running. Most of us, all the time. We are tri-athletes unknowingly in training. Phew. How tiring . . .

We all have too much to do, high expectations of ourselves, and too little time — or so it seems. Many of us go to bed at night reviewing what we didn't do, and unfortunately feeling stressed or like a failure. We must stop this madness now! This chapter will teach you a new way of looking at your relationship with your work environment and with yourself, and present immediately useful life skills and concepts that can put you back in the driver's seat — right now — and then, keep you there. Sound good? You bet! Read on . . .

Driver = Staying in Charge of Ourselves
Versus
Driven = Wearing out our Irreplaceable Parts

As a psychologist and international authority on many forms of stress and its effects on us, one of my logos and life missions is to "Save our Human-Ware." I think about the human condition and how to make things better, in all sorts of ways — all the time. It is who I am, what I do, and what my life is all about. I know that we cannot upgrade *our* worn out parts as we do our hardware and software. We can't buy a new us at *Good Guy's* or *Best Buy*. So we must treat our bodies, minds, and spirits with the utmost respect and care.

This chapter will show you how to work smarter, not harder. And my piece of the pie in this terrific book of wisdom is to show you, "How to Stay the Driver . . . Not the Driven." I am continually, both personally and professionally, striving to do everything I teach you. Just because I have a Ph.D., other advanced degrees and licenses, and scads of education does not protect me from being human. Besides, I don't want protection. I like being human. I walk the same paths as you. Here is one of my all-time favorite quotes I came across early in graduate school:

> *"We are all more simply human than otherwise."*
>
> — Harry Stack Sullivan

What this means to me is that no matter who we are, what we do or have done, we are all part of the global human condition. What affects one of us is more than likely to be affecting most of us. I have always found this idea deeply meaningful because it connects us to each other no matter what.

So every time I write, I write for me to learn as well as for you. I strive to practice what I preach, doing so imperfectly at times like everyone else, but I keep on . . . keeping on.

You and those in your world deserve the best possible life experience, along with the best possible you. Life is a constant learning experience — whether we like it or not. If we choose to fully participate, which means being "awake" or "present," life's lessons and opportunities are bountiful. This is what makes life challenging, fun, and fascinating. We can choose to see ourselves and our environments as an ever-changing and ever-growing positive, upward spiral, or we can complain, hide, and whine.

Life's lessons aren't always pleasant, I can assure you! But living them and learning from them can raise you to a higher level of functioning and knowing, which is a great feeling indeed. I love this quote:

"Anyone who stops learning is old,
whether at twenty or eighty.
Anyone who keeps learning stays young.
The greatest thing in life is to keep your mind young."

— Henry Ford

So, start reaching for your personal brass ring, today, tomorrow and every day thereafter. Believe me, you are worth it! And so are those around you that you love and who love you.

Being driven affects us all.

We share common as well as individualized reactions. Some common reactions (which we may or might not notice) are:

- Being a grump.
- Thinking less clearly.
- Processing information incompletely; e.g., not listening to what others tell you, not fully listening to messages, or not answering completely what we are asked.
- Eating more than is good for us, not eating, or eating in a hurry.
- Not thinking things through.
- Making impulsive decisions (including spending $$) and taking quicker actions.
- Isolating ourselves from others in various ways.
- Using more alcohol and/or prescription medications, along with illegal substances, to numb our stress and keep going.
- Blaming others more often for things that go wrong.

If you aren't sure which ones sound like you, ask your co-workers, friends, or significant others. Use the quick checklist. They may see what you can't. That's okay; that's what friends are for. True friends are willing to help keep us in better shape. Why? They love us, and then we make better friends for them. So it is truly a win/win situation.

I have separated the chapter into three of the more typical areas in which we often become lost, frustrated, overwhelmed, and therefore driven. These are life arenas where we can learn to work smarter, not harder.

- Using Technology and Ending the TechnoStress it Brings
- The Home Office — Dreams and Realities
- Get a Life — and Keep It

In each area I offer ideas and tips about "Staying the Driver." It is time to realize your dreams. Dreams can come true, and setting boundaries, having clear goals, and taking action allow these areas of your life to be experienced with greater joy. Let's get going!

Living a 24/7 Lifestyle????!!!! Egads!

Using Technology and Ending the TechnoStress it Brings

Technology is clearly changing the way we live and affecting the way we relate to ourselves and others, though not necessarily for the better. Technology can cause stress for those of us who use it, as well as for those around us. I called the result *TechnoStress,* and wrote a whole book on the topic (*TechnoStress: Coping With Technology @Work @Home @Play,* John Wiley and Sons, 1997). We need to understand not only what technology can do *for* us, but what it is doing *to* us — and how to remedy the unforeseen difficulties it brings.

Sure, you are wired, but it is not the caffeine that may be driving you. A large part of it is technology. Day and night, connected to a computer, cellphone, pager, fax, e-mail and voice mail, it is difficult (but not impossible) to escape feeling "on call." We succumb to the pressure to be available 24 hours a day, seven days a week. Today many vacations simply just mean staying connected to work from some other location. Webster's Dictionary defines vacation as *a period of rest from work, study.* It certainly would be nice to get back to that experience, wouldn't it?

Today, we are clearly *working harder,* ***not*** *smarter.* Let's look at some of the effects we feel in today's work environment, which are all the more complicated by what *TechnoStress* brings into play.

> *"Though more and more people are choosing to use certain forms of technology, TechnoStress across the board is on the increase. Whether people are intimidated by technology or love technology — or are somewhere in the middle — they feel more stress because of Boundary Invasion and Multitasking Madness."*
>
> — Dr. Michelle M. Weil, *Workforce Magazine*

Typical Responses in Today's Work Environment

As the international expert on TechnoStress and how it interacts with all areas of our lives, I can honestly tell you that it is a world-wide phenomenon that no one anticipated. Upwards of 90 percent of the population experience some degree of technological "dis-ease," so if you relate to this information, remember:

You Are Not Alone.

Here are the behavioral experiences of today:

The Bottom Line

We experience less of these great attributes:

- Performance
- Productivity
- Efficiency

- Job Satisfaction

-and-

We experience more of these not-so-great attributes:

- Resistance and Avoidance
- Absenteeism and Attrition
- Job-Related Stress
- Anxiety and Depression

"In the end, addressing TechnoStress is a commercial imperative. The industry has exhausted the supply of buyers willing to put up with complex and alienating products."

— Peter McGrath,
Senior Editor, *Newsweek*

Rx for TechnoStress

One of my passions for the past twenty plus years has been to show people how to live and work with technology while preserving their irreplaceable human-ware. I am pleased that highly respected corporations, governments and countries around the globe, along with the media, have taken this issue seriously. *Newsweek, Forbes, Business Week, Investors Business Daily, The National Safety Council, Workforce Magazine*, and more have featured this topical, growing area of new stress. The powers that be are concerned for our well-being.

For example, this topic is so important *Newsweek* magazine devoted an entire issue to what technology is doing to our lives. The entire magazine was entitled: *e-Life*.

"Users take the glitches personally because of the perception that technology never fails."

— Dr. Michelle Weil

Here are some handy tools for your use as needed. I call them *Technostress Busters:*

- Be Aware of your own TechnoStress.
- Know that it is not about your inadequacies!
- Let on — tell others.
- Develop an empowered attitude.
- Take care of yourself physically and emotionally.
- Ask for help and accept only clear answers.
- Be a tenacious advocate for yourself.

Here are some handy resolutions to use daily. Think of these as personal mantras. The results can be positively staggering!

Personal and Professional Resolutions
-or-
How to Stay the Driver . . . Not the Driven

- Technology is a tool for my use.
- Technology will have problems.
- When technology fails, I will not take it personally. I can find assistance and solutions.
- I measure my technological competence by what I know, not by what I don't know.
- I have the right to control access to me so that I can stay creative and productive.
- Technology can work 24 hours a day, 7 days a week. *But I do not!*
- Technology never needs to rest or play. *But I do.*
- I need to spend time away from technology. *And I will!*

The Home Office — Dreams and Realities

Working from Home: Harder Can Become Smarter

Your computer is a multitasking machine. It can simultaneously track your e-mail, do word processing, facilitate web surfing, and more.

Humans can multitask, but the more we do, the less efficient we become. It is important to stop our own multitasking madness. When we do, we stay focused and feel fulfilled while reducing our body's physiological and psychological overload.

Others access us when they wish. Our pagers beep, our cellphones ring, our e-mail arrives with a hearty "You've Got Mail" at all times of the day and night. We are feeling inundated by requests, communications, and information and have lost our sense of self in the process. With more than twenty-five years of experience as a clinical psychologist, consultant, and "technologist," I believe it is imperative to stay sane and human amidst this technological bombardment. And we can!

Today, our very survival depends on our ability to set effective limits and manage this avalanche of information. Ending information overload is but one of the roads to fulfillment. Here are some tips for making it work for you!

Staying Human in our Technological World: Ending Home Office Boundary Invasion and Information Overload

Tips

- Use your recording devices (voice mail, answering machine, etc.) to say when you are and are not available.
- Do not change your work voice mail daily. Make a generic one and change it only if out of town.
- Leave word when you are unavailable and when you will be returning calls.
- Find out what your phone company offers as new services that might assist you in your business. For example, get a voice mail system so people don't experience a busy signal when they call.
- Put notes on your door, or make open/closed door policies regarding interruptions.
- Use signs, orange cones, etc., to let the kids and others know

when you are at work and are not to be disturbed.

- Use an open door policy when others can come in.
- Turn off ringers on fax machines and other equipment to allow you to stay focused and eliminate interrupted phone conversations and dictations.
- Unplug when you can. In other words, turn off and tune out. Know when you are "off."

Here are some notices to post on the wall, or give to others as needed.

Your Home Office Bill of Rights

1. I am the boss, not my technology.
2. I decide when to use the tools technology provides.
3. I have the right to choose what technology to use and what to put aside.
4. I can use technology to stay informed, connected, and productive, in my own way.
5. When technology has problems, I will be prepared to handle them.
6. Technology can work 24/7, but I choose when to begin and when to stop working.
7. Technology never needs to eat, but I do.
8. I can work successfully at home by enforcing my boundary needs with others.
9. I will ensure I go outside, play, rest, and remember to actively honor all my human needs.
10. I will constantly affirm what I accomplish and not worry about what I do not get done.

Get a Life — and Keep It

Better Living through Technology: From Disneyland to Technoland

Radio took 38 years to reach an audience of 50,000,000; television took 13 years; the personal computer took 16; and the Internet took only 4! Now we have Ethernet and more. As technological advances spiral into our new millennium, we are witness to unprecedented growth in new technologies only dreamed about before.

At the 1964 World's Fair in New York, General Electric sponsored the *Carousel of Progress*. Its theme song promised us "Oh it's a great big beautiful tomorrow, shining at the end of everyday . . ." and ended up in a long-term exhibit at Anaheim's Disneyland for many years. Way back when (before they removed the exhibit), visitors were titillated by colorful visions of how much brighter, easier, and time-efficient the future would be because of technology.

Well, that's Disneyland for you.

Why do you think they have one area called "Fantasyland?"

Tech support or not

Unfortunately, the service at help desks or tech support people at work or on the phone don't always provide the service you are hoping for, or even speak English. Oftentimes there are long, incomprehensible voice mail systems to traverse, which only add to your stress.

Welcome to today's Carousel of Technoland. Rather than traveling in circles (as the ride took us), here are some handy ideas.

Working Smarter in Today's Technoland

1. Before buying any product, try out the tech support number and see what you receive. Use this response as a determining factor in purchasing that piece of technology.
2. You will be encouraged by most major tech support lines to go

to their "easy-to-use" website. Don't do it! This ploy is simply a money and manpower saver for the company. Getting to live people quickly is still your best bet and keeps you the driver.

3. Keep pressing "0" or pretend you have a rotary phone when given the choice. It will get you a real human faster, and there are no rotary phone police who will come knocking on your door!
4. When you get a live person, briefly tell him or her your problem and ask if this person is equipped to help before going too far into your difficulties or questions.
5. Be assertive, and never be concerned about asking to be transferred to someone with more time on the job, who speaks clearer, or who seems nicer than what the random button-push sent your way.
6. Once in the system with a live, helpful person, ask what the default numbers are for their complex voice mail systems (they all have them). Then you will know how to more quickly reach a human in the future. Additionally, tell the person that if you get cut off, you want him or her to call you back. Give out your number and get a commitment for a call back.

It's time to learn to "Tech It Easy"

Using the above ideas will help you access, create boundaries, and take time to smell the real roses, not just those virtual ones you see on a website.

Developing Emotional Muscle

I like to think of this concept as becoming emotionally sturdy or hardy. I use this often with the patients I see, as well as my corporate and sales consulting clients. *You'll not be the least surprised when I tell you 'tis not an easy world we live in.*

This is why being involved in saving our human-ware is quite important to me — so are my last two book chapters and events such as my upcoming keynote address in Kentucky. In May 2004, I have the honor and privilege to present my ideas on coping with stress to high-ranking members of our government, FBI, and national security personnel at the prestigious *Terrorism 2004: The American Community Preparedness Conference.*

For this very reason, my esteemed colleagues and I each authored a chapter in the recent book, *Maintain Balance in an Unsteady World* (September 2003). Talk about timely self-help and wake-up call publications and presentations! This is where America and each and every one of us human beings needs to spend time looking within and around us, and learn to apply these principles for **today**.

Never in our history has there been a greater need to become hearty in our spirit, actions, and attitudes, and do what it takes!

"Knowing is not enough, we must apply.
Willing is not enough, we must do."

— Johann von Goethe

Your personal and professional results will be dramatic. The sky is the limit here, and the choice is yours. I hope you use what I offer in these pages to make it a great moment, a terrific day, your best year ever, and beyond. Please enjoy this chapter again and again. Pass the information along and create an upward spiral of growth. Remember:

Stay the Driver . . . not the Driven

The DMV, me and the world, have
placed **YOU** behind the wheel for a reason!

Happy Motoring.

About Michelle M. Weil, Ph.D.

Dr. Michelle Weil is a Professional Keynote Speaker, Corporate Consultant, Clinical Psychologist, the "Miss Manners of Technology," and author of the books TechnoStress: Coping With Technology @Work @Home @Play, *which teaches you how to thrive in the age of high-tech, and* The Mental Health Technology Bible. *In September 2003, she wrote a chapter entitled "Designing Boundaries at Work, Home and Play" in the book,* Maintain Balance in an Unsteady World. *Featured from "Good Morning America" to the* Wall Street Journal, *she is sought after for her commentary on resolving the stress that is created in our lives and by our lifestyles.*

Dr. Weil is a consistent contributor in professional and popular journals and magazines. She was recently featured by the San Diego Tribune *and authored "Rx for TechnoStress" in NSA's* Professional Speaker Magazine *(May 2003). She published the article entitled "Stop, Breathe and Think — It's Time," in the* National Psychologist *(July/August, 2003), and was honored to be the closing Keynote at the prestigious* Terrorism 2004: American Community Preparedness Conference *May 11-13, 2004.*

Through extensive media coverage along with her role as National Spokesperson for MCI, Activision and others, Dr. Weil has reached millions with her message and her wisdom. She heads the consulting firm Human-Ware, LLC, is an avid speaker, trainer and writer, maintains a private clinical psychology practice, and is the mother of two teenage children (yikes!).

Contact Information:
Michelle M. Weil, Ph.D.
Human-Ware, LLC
Phone: (760) 730-3894
E-Mail: Weil@Human-Ware.com
Website: www.Human-Ware.com

Without Your Head, You're Dead

by Louis B. Cady, M.D.

The care, feeding, and driving of one's own brain is both ridiculously easy as well as extremely complex. Perhaps the best explanation starts with a flashback to an old episode of the comedy, *Gomer Pyle: USMC.*

In the episode in question, Gomer was assigned to take charge of the PX on base when the quartermaster was out sick. He promptly reorganized the entire store into his own homespun categories of "animal, vegetable, or mineral." Although his classification scheme was not "official Marine Corps issue," it was, nevertheless, a useful attempt to impose order on a confusing array of choices . . . at least for Gomer.

Based on my training in psychiatry, a decade in private practice, and monitoring my own successes (and failures) in keeping up and keeping pace, I think that a very useful categorization scheme for the care and feeding of one's own psyche — and life — is a similar tripartite organizational scheme: biological, cognitive, and behavioral.

This is not just some artificial scheme that some nerdy psychiatrist in an ivory tower dreamed up. And by the way, here's a word up front about why you should be reading what a shrink has to say, whether or not you think you're the most un-neurotic, nonconflicted, happy-go-lucky guy or gal to ever put on a business suit or uniform. I've seen every little human foible and frailty pushed to the limit. You say you've got problems with procrastination? I see people's careers ruined by it. You've occasionally told little teeny-tiny white lies? I've seen lives, marriages, careers, and companies destroyed because of them. You go to work with the sniffles? I've seen people who would have died if I hadn't insisted that their cancer get diagnosed and treated.

Do you have a problem being absent-minded? I can tell you what this seemingly mildly annoying difficulty may stem from, and what you can do to banish it from your life, ***forever.***

Are you tired? We can talk about some medical conditions that you may never have heard of that are slowly killing you. And you don't even know it.

In other words, I can, and I will, tell you in this chapter what the tiny defects in your performance, efficiency, and energy levels may ***really*** be indicating, because in my psychiatric and medical practice, I've seen all of them taken to the limit.

Let's start at the beginning. Psychiatry got its start with an interesting guy, whose original research interest was the sex organs of eels. His name was Sigmund Freud. And his goal was nothing less than the mechanical and methodical understanding of the human mind on purely biological grounds. Along the way, his course detoured dramatically, and he ended his career plumbing the depths of the human unconscious mind . . . and no longer contemplating eel sex organs.

In Freud's footsteps, the practice of psychiatry and psychology was organized along the study of the mind: of one's ***psychology***. In the middle part of the 20th century, the "behaviorists" came along and decided that it really didn't matter what you ***thought*** or if you were "conflicted;" it only mattered what you ***did***. "Change your behavior, change your psychology," was their reasoning. Hence, the ***behavioral*** approach came into being.

Now, being upstanding, card-carrying members of the "Prozac generation," we know that it's those pesky neurotransmitters that get out of whack that cause all of our problems. We have entered the ***biological*** orientation of psychiatry.

Of course, like the three blind men feeling different parts of the elephant, the informed and integrated health care practitioner knows it's not, as technological expert Daniel Burrus notes, "either/or;" it is instead, a choice of "both/and." And in the case of running your brain effectively, it is ***all three***.

OK, I hear you asking. What does all of this stuff have to do with ***me?***

The simple truth is that you would never have picked up this book if you were happy as a clam, sipping a refreshing tropical libation, and contemplating an idyllic beach somewhere with money in the bank to live on for life and no pressing obligations. This is a book for the movers and the shakers: the people who are actively engaged in life and who, in the early 21st century, are now among the most overworked, right-sized, techno-savvy, media frazzled, Wi-Fi'ed, and Starbucks-caffeinated generation ever to inhabit the planet. Like the old Charlie Chaplin flick where the hapless worker is able to crank widgets on the assembly line until the assembly line picks up speed, we've done alright until now. Unfortunately, the pace has picked up and is continuing to accelerate.

Nowhere is this more evident than in the lives of my patients, and in the lives of those strangers I meet when I am traveling for business. This perspective — and the tripartite model I shared with you a few paragraphs back — is the "news from the front" I wish to share with you.

Just for a moment, imagine a carpenter building a house. To know how to build a house, but not to build it, is a defect in behavior. To not know how to build a house, but to try to go ahead and build one anyway, would represent a defect in one's knowledge, or, in this case, one's psychology. And to both know how to build a house, and to start to build a house, but then to run out of energy: that would be a defect in one's underlying biology. Let's start with the mind, and our understanding of the way we are and the way we think.

Psychology

One's ***psychology***, or the way one sees life, is crucial. Motivational authorities including Zig Ziglar, Jim Rohn, and Brian Tracy all pound home the point. From a utilitarian point of view, it ultimately comes down to a choice that you have to make: "what is the most workable philosophy?" [Note: see the web sources listed at the end of the chapter for more details on these references and multiple other topics to follow in this chapter.]

A dysfunctional philosophy, one guaranteed to beget failure, is this: "There's no point. The world's a terrible place. People are just nasty and dishonest. Life ain't fair. There's no point in trying. You can't fight City Hall. The deck is stacked against me."

Come on. Can you imagine strapping on your business duds and going out into the world to transact business with that poisonous attitude?

A more neutral attitude would be: "On balance, life is fair. I'll probably get back what I put out. Therefore, I'll give everything a reasonable effort."

You'll probably get a much more reasonable return on your efforts.

Imagine the alternative: a relentlessly upbeat attitude. "Wow! I wonder what exciting opportunities I'll have today? I can hardly wait to start the day! Whatever I deal with today, I'm sure I'll do just fine."

Because of the principle of ***reciprocity*** — that is, people tend to give back what they receive — your business interactions with people will be immeasurably improved with this third, and more adaptive stance. I've proved it in my own life, and I've seen my patients prove it in their lives in the course of their therapy.

In fact, there is a school of psychotherapy known as *cognitive therapy*. It identifies an incredibly important "cognitive triad" that is just as important for psychiatric patients as it is for average Jane's and Joe's out there who are having a tough time at work.

The *cognitive triad* principle is simple. There's an event, a perception, and a reaction. For example: someone doesn't show for an appointment with you. You ***perceive*** this situation as a personal rejection. You ***react*** emotionally. And it could ruin the rest of your day.

A more adaptive way to deal with unexpected woes is to studiously choose your perception. An alternative way to view the appointment which didn't occur is: "Oh, well, he probably just forgot about it." You could even accept some responsibility and learn from it. In casting about for explanations, you would do well to consider what your ***own*** contribution was. Perhaps you could have called ahead?

Please don't get me wrong. There's already enough stress in most of our lives without needlessly being made to feel worse about our own contributions to our misfortunes. But as Harvey Mackay once dryly noted: "The best place to find a helping hand. . . . is at the end of your arm."

Recently, I was riding in the car of a pharmaceutical representative. The company that had hired me for the occasion had paid good money to get my bod to parts northeast in order to give a luncheon and dinner talk, as well as to motor around with the rep and call on physicians. The luncheon came off as scheduled; everything else was a disaster. Doctors were out of their offices. Some were too busy. Not enough people had responded positively for the dinner. It was cancelled.

As we rode around in her car, she railed against how "they should have been more responsible; they should have let me know that they wouldn't have time today to see us. After all, I called them earlier this week." Yes, but she hadn't called ***that day***.

The problem with blaming other people for your every misfortune is, of course, that if it is ***you*** that's the source of your own misfortunes, you'll never realize it because you're so busy blaming everyone else!

Let's get back to that cognitive triad. The event: doctors are not available. The perception: "those irresponsible doctors; they should have known better. How irresponsible of them (and, by the way, there's nothing I could have done about it anyway)." The emotional reaction: anger and being upset.

Here's an alternative view. The event: doctors are not available. The perception: "Hmm, I know they're busy, and, after all, I didn't call to confirm the appointment. That's why it didn't come off." The emotional reaction: neutral, or, perhaps, rueful. The exciting thing: the presence of a take-home message! "Hmmmm. I have identified a deficiency in my sales technique and appointment-making style. Perhaps if I had called in advance to confirm, the doctors would have been available."

Unfortunately, you will never get to this clear-headed state if you just let your perceptions and emotions run away with you.

David Burns, in his excellent book, *Feeling Good: The New Mood Therapy*, lists some of the more common cognitive distortions. At the risk of harping on the hapless pharmaceutical rep, let me take that situation and run through some of these distortions. Keep in mind that in order to ***really*** do these distortions up right, you have to begin your dysfunctional statement with the dependent clause, "In my all-knowing, omniscient, and God-like knowledge and power, I know that . . ." and then just fill in the blank. Let's have some fun and do some. I'll list the technical name of the distortion first, then give you an example.

- Mind-reading — "In my all-knowing, omniscient (etc.) way, I know that they didn't really want to see me today. That's why they stood me up."
- "Fortune telling" or "predicting the future" — "Gee whiz, it's always going to be like this. They'll always be standing me up. Why even try?"

- Catastrophizing — "This ruins my entire day. Nothing else matters."
- "Mental filter" (seeing just the negative) — "Forget about the great sales call I just had with the doc. That receptionist surely was unpleasant."

You can quickly see that going through the day with this mentally poisonous routine would ruin it!

Here's Doc Cady's down-home way to counteract the mental poisons: identify the problem, then run it through ***The Five P's.*** Here's how.

Throughout the day, take the smallest, cheapest hand-held recorder you can obtain with you. When something occurs that really steams your veggies, make a voice note of it. Example: "I'm really annoyed that those doctors flaked out on me when I set up an appointment." That's it. No long and introspective circumlocutions: just a quick little verbal note. Let's say another thing that went wrong is a physician didn't listen to you particularly well —and this happens to both reps and patients! Make a note.

At the end of the day, take your microcassette tape or digital recording, play it one time, and carefully write down what's bugging you, at the top of ***one*** page of paper. *Write only one "downer" per page.* This is the toxin. It's now time to construct the anti-venom. Take a deep breath. Flip back to your first page.

The first step is to determine what's ***pertinent***. What are the facts? The doc stood you up for an appointment, let's say, or your major client didn't call you back. That's what happened. But what was ***your*** contribution? Let's say you didn't call to confirm in advance. That's what's pertinent. Write it down.

Step two is what's ***personal***. In other words, what can you ***personally*** do about the situation? You talk to the client on the telephone in advance! Write it down.

Step three is ***proactive.*** In other words, it's up to you. YOU have to take an action, or series of actions, in advance to get what you want. Make the list!

Step four, figure out what that action will be, and what the results will look like, in a ***positive*** fashion. This is incredibly important. In other words, don't visualize it, or articulate it like this: "In order to keep my scumbag clients from canceling out on me at the last minute, I guess I gotta..." This is the blame game, and it's for losers. Instead, conceptualize a positive outcome: "In order to have the privilege and opportunity to represent my product in a maximally productive way, I . . ."

Finally, step five. Articulate your vision in the ***present tense.***

Here's where it gets interesting. You're not done yet. Review the notes you made, then craft a custom made affirmation for yourself in order to deal with every frustration and personal outrage of the day. Remember that you have to accept responsibility for your share. This doesn't mean you have to accept responsibility for a mugging, or for your business burning down. But let's say you get cut off in traffic by a pushy driver. Why is it eating on you so much? Maybe because you're running behind too. Maybe you didn't get up early enough. Maybe you're over-committed and overwhelmed, and your life has to go *perfectly* in order for you to not be stressed! If you'd been happy as a clam motoring on down the road, chilled, groovin' to your favorite tunes on the radio and not white-knuckling it to get to the next appointment, maybe the pushy chap wouldn't have discombobulated you and rained on your parade!

Back to business. Let's look at your 5 P's. We'll continue using my hapless pharmaceutical rep acquaintance as an example.

Here's a pertinent, personal, positive, proactive and present tense affirmation: "In order for me to be able to sell my incredibly valuable product [positive], and so that my appointment will be secure with Dr.

X [pertinent and proactive], I will [personal and proactive] call in advance on the day of the appointment so that I will have the opportunity to adequately explain such-and-such [positive]. In this manner, the sales presentation and the opportunity will take care of itself [positive!]."

If all you did was just sit down at the end of the day, make this list, craft your affirmations, and run through them one time, you would be ahead of the competition. But you really want to ***Work Smarter, Not Harder***, don't you? Then you need the ultra super-duper luxo-version of the above.

After you write down your statement encompassing the **Five P's,** *you record your statement.* You can do this on a cheap audio cassette recorder which you can take with you in your car. In order to get the best possible results, my recommendations are that you record a sentence at a time, with a pause after every sentence so that you can repeat your words aloud while you're listening. You can play the tape in your car, or play it in your bathroom while you're getting dressed for work. You could do both!

By contrast, here's what the losers mumble to themselves trudging away from another missed appointment on the way to their cars. "Awhh, it happened again. [pertinent!] They did it to me again [avoidance of personal responsibility]. I don't know what I can do about it [abdication of proactive stance]. Gee, if this kind of garbage continues to happen [certainly no positive notions here], I don't know if I'll ever be able to garner any kind of success with this company [future orientation, neatly combined with "fortune telling" and "catastrophizing"].

The contrast between these two paradigms is nowhere more crisply defined than by Prof. W.W. Broadbent, M.D., Ph.D., at the University of Southern California Medical Center: "The major way of doing anything with one's self is to ***own one's self***. This means to *take full responsibility and accountability for whatever I am doing at any moment*, with anybody. It means, among other things, that I get rid of all the extra fingers that I point at people and situations to explain my behavior. When a person says, 'He made me mad,' that is not accurate. It is 'I made me mad.' When I permit myself the luxury of taking that full responsibility, then I'm on first base, at least, because then I can do something about it."

The sad thing is, some people trudge through their entire business and personal lives saying "other people made me mad" and "other people stood me up for appointments." Is it any wonder that with the increased pace of business, coupled with the fact that people are never really taught how to "run their brains" either by their parents or in school, that there's such an epidemic of depression, anxiety and obesity in society today?

Behavioral

The idiocy of a totally focused "behavioral" approach to solving problems is nowhere more clearly demonstrated than in W. Edwards Deming's famous "red bead" exercise. The gist of the scenario is that participants at his seminars were asked to dip a paddle with indentations in it into a container of white beads with a few red beads mixed in and then pull out their paddles containing only white beads. When people were obviously unable to succeed, he would exhort them with cries of "Try harder!" or "We need to reconfigure and re-engineer the team!" or "Maybe we need to fire the incompetents!"

The message, obviously, was that it was the *system that was flawed, not the people*. Indeed, Professor Russell L. Ackoff, at Wharton Business School, notes: "To manage a system effectively, you might focus on the interactions of the parts rather than their behavior taken separately." So a total "behaviorist" approach to *working smarter, not harder*, will not — ultimately — be smarter. It may be harder!

Nevertheless, like our lazy carpenter friend, if we know how to build the house but don't pick up the hammer, we won't make much progress.

Here are some tips I've shared with some of my patients and which I use in my own life. This is not the "ABC's" of behavioral management. It is the "**ABCDEFG's.**" Let's take a look.

A is for AWARENESS. In a sense, that's the "psychology" section we just completed. "The ultimate value of life depends upon awareness," commented Aristotle, "and the power of contemplation rather than upon mere survival." The Doc Cady version of the great philosopher's message is: "You've got to be aware of the problem of getting stood up for appointments (or whatever) or you won't sell many widgets!"

B is for BELIEF. This is actually pretty simple for anyone who is not psychotic. If you're psychotic, then you have more problems than I can deal with in this book. But for most rational folks, the simple commonsensical beliefs are enough. ***If what you do is positive, you'll get positive results back***, and ***if what you do is negative, you'll get negative results back***.

Insult the customer, get turned out on your ear. Be nice to the customer, get more business. Lose appointments? Starve. Get appointments? Have more chances for success. Don't use a planner? Be disorganized. Don't sell much. Starve (again!). Use a planner? Be organized. Plan your strategies. Secure the appointments. And have more chances for success.

C is for CONCEPTUALIZATION. In this case, ***conceptualization*** is a noun that calls for you to ***do*** something. The noun form, or "thing" is what you form in your mind about what's causing your success (or lack of it). But that's only half the story. For the unsuccessful pharmaceutical rep, the original "conceptualization" was that "the doctors are irresponsible and are not following through on their appointments with me." *The successful conceptualization must involve a behavior.* That is, you sit down, reason the situation through, and formulate the most adaptive or positive *conceptualization* you can muster; then you affirm it onto a tape recorder. If you're really techno-savvy, a digital or mp3 file will also work well. The bottom line: in order to have your conceptualization, you must **conceptualize**. *You must do something in your head.*

D is for DO IT and DOCUMENT IT! "He only earns his freedom and his life who takes them every day by storm," commented Johann Wolfgang von Goethe. More colloquially, like our edified but behaviorally challenged carpenter, you've got to pick up your hammer and start pounding nails if you know how to build a house . . . and if you ever want to live in it or sell it. You also get to serve as your own "construction foreman." In order to know how your building is coming, you need progress reports. You need to know what's coming up tomorrow, and the day after that, and the week after that. You need to know where your next job is coming from. You need contact information for your suppliers and customers. In other words, you need *a planner.*

The most successful thing I've ever done with patients who are mired in helplessness and hopelessness in order to get them off the dime is to have them *document what they are doing*. Like the Heisenberg "Uncertainty Principle," the very act of observing a phenomenon changes it. If you have to write down in your planner, regarding your day's activities, "missed every appointment because no one was there," then even the most business-challenged among us would recognize that there is a common theme here and perhaps we should learn the tune.

The flip side is that when we ***commit to action*** and ***get results***, we also need to have that written down. By so doing, we can experience the Law of Cause and Effect again, and internalize it at our deepest level. This law, according to Doc Cady, is, "You do what you need to do and you get the goodies. You don't do what you know you need to do, and you won't be getting the goodies." ***Documenting it*** allows us to celebrate our success and what got us there.

E is for Expect Results! This gets easier as time passes and you DO IT more and DOCUMENT IT more. As it becomes clear that your results are coming directly from the efforts you're putting forth, it becomes much easier to trust, on faith, that you have every right to ***expect results*** — and good ones at that — from your efforts. There are many wonderful books and audio programs available which will put you in a mindset of "positive self-expectancy" and allow you to expect positive results in the future before you even achieve them, based on anecdote after anecdote, and case study after case study. Eventually, if you just keep putting enough of the good stuff in, your negative self-talk will be pummeled into submission.

FAILURE is to be Expected. I love what the relentlessly upbeat Zig Ziglar has to say about failure. "Failure is an event . . . it's not a person. Yesterday is a cancelled check. Today is a brand new day, and it's yours!" Look. Given that this is not a perfect world, and "the system" does not always give back to you perfectly what you put into it, you will occasionally encounter unexpected failures and setbacks. Expect them to occur occasionally, just as you expect your good results. After these occasional mishaps rock your world, put them behind you and go on. Pop in a motivational audio. Read some good books. Dissect the event dispassionately; see if there are things you can learn from it. Then move on!

G is for GO BACK and keep trying. One previously severely ill patient with whom I have worked for almost a decade has struggled for the last four years to get her ex-husband to pay her what's her due in a divorce settlement, has struggled to get him to pay her kids' medical expenses, has taken personal bankruptcy, wrangled with the IRS, suffered woes with a string of lawyers and has not unexpectedly teetered close to suicide many times. I kept focusing on having her go back and keep trying. We went through every letter you just read: ***A*** through ***F***. Failures kept occurring —some through lack of knowledge on her part, and some because she didn't have the biological strength to fight. She persisted. She kept going back. And she is now winning big. Her life and those of her two children are radically improving.

I have had some patients who have not gone back and kept trying. The most severe of these cases of personal suffering are now dead by their own hand. The human tragedy is that suicide is a permanent solution to what, upon closer inspection, is almost always a temporary problem. It is an emotional decision, founded on false logic, and predicated upon almost unbelievable psychological pain and agony.

The alternative is to **GO BACK** and keep trying. I've never had a case where it didn't work.

Biological

Greg Anderson, an NBA forward/center for the San Antonio Spurs and the Atlanta Hawks, has cogently observed that, "The concept of total wellness recognizes that our every thought, word, and behavior affects our greater health and well-being. And we, in turn, are affected not only emotionally but also physically and spiritually."

He is profoundly correct, and his statement should indelibly cement the connection between your **psychology**, your **behavior,** and your **biological state.**

Renee Descartes, the philosopher, not a basketball player, has caused much devilment with his notion of the "dichotomy" of the mind/body connection. Essentially, his position was that the mind didn't affect the body and the body didn't affect the mind: they were autonomous. Wrong!

We can see this now on functional brain images, where actual changes occur in our biology based on what we think. Over a decade ago, Konrad Schwartz at UCLA did some groundbreaking work on this with functional brain imaging and what he termed "cognitive bio-behavioral therapy." He was actually able to show changes in brain activity based on his therapeutic model. This experiment showed why psychotherapy had been able to get people better before any of the antidepressants were introduced in the mid-twentieth century. "Change your thoughts, change your mood, and you change your underlying brain biology," was the way it worked.

So far, we've talked about changing both your thoughts and your behaviors. In psychiatry, we know that increasingly excellent medications can, on a purely biological basis, change your thoughts — lifting you out of a depressive state, for example — and then with therapy you can change your behaviors. Thus, the mind-body duo works both ways in terms of cause and effect.

Here's the rub. It doesn't matter how positive you are in your psychology, or how willing you are to engage in the appropriate behaviors if your body answers your call to achievement with, "I just can't."

The all too often result, which is a tragedy, really, is that the hapless victim of his or her biology concludes — wrongly — that she/he is just being "lazy," or "scatterbrained," or "unmotivated" and that "it's hopeless" and "I'll never be able to change."

Over and over again, I've seen good men and women who come in to my practice with undiagnosed medical problems. Sometimes the "psychiatric problems" they present me with are either entirely medical in origin (hypothyroidism, for example, masquerading as depression) or else are medical issues strongly compounding their psychiatric conditions.

Some of what I'm about to list will be controversial; some won't. [Check the web resources for further details.]

Attention Deficit Disorder — (with or without being "hyper"). I'm starting with this one for two reasons: (1) I see it more in entrepreneurs than in any other patient population — and the target audience for this book will have a highly entrepreneurial mindset. (2) If you are feeling the need to "Work Smarter and Not Harder" then you either think you're working dumb or not hard enough. In either case, "ADD" may be the culprit.

Estimates for the percentages of this condition in the United States range from 4 to 8 percent of children. The rate is fairly consistent across the world. (It's not a "U.S. condition.") It's so intensely biologically inherited, it's almost tied with height as determined purely on a genetic basis. (In other words, you can't "catch it" or have MTV "infect you.") About half of these kids continue to have some difficulty as adults. This doesn't mean that adults with ADD are "hyper" or that they're globally inattentive. But they might be endless procrastinators, lose things easily, get behind constantly, or be easily frustrated and even explosive at times. (If any of this applies to you, you may have the sense that you need to work smarter ***and*** harder!) Medication works, and is now considered appropriate in adults.

Anxiety disorders — rampant in our society. If you're quivering in your boots, you won't be successful in making appointments or keeping them. Non-addicting, non-"dope-you-up" medication strategies are available. Do yourself a favor and find out about them.

Depression — Most people know about this one. It's currently estimated that 6 percent, or 13 million Americans, suffer from depression each year. Only 1 out of 4 get adequate treatment. Not surprisingly, it's the number one leading cause of disability and costs the economy an incredible 30 ***billion*** dollars a year in lost productivity.

I estimate that a considerably higher number than 6 percent of the readers of this book will have depression or a variant of it, simply because of the nature of the book. Again, anyone who feels the need to "work smarter, not harder" is already stressed, and stress tends to bring on depression if you're vulnerable. It doesn't mean that you're weak or a wimp; it may mean that you've got too much on your plate. Help is available.

Quickly, here are some medical conditions which can nail you:

- **"Adrenal burnout:"** This is the stress disease of the late 20th and early 21st century. Your adrenal glands sit on top of your kidneys and pump out hormones to help you deal with stress, inflammation, and sugar and salt balance. Felt any stress lately? Felt nothing but stress lately? Perhaps you're essentially a happy, cheerful, motivated person, but it feels like somebody has pulled the plug on your energy. Easy laboratory evaluation is available, including some which can be done just using your saliva. Treatment by a holistic and sophisticated medical practitioner can restore your energy.
- **Hypothyroidism:** I have seen this diagnosis, as well as its treatment, butchered repeatedly by well meaning practitioners. The typical difficulties are checking only an indirect measurement of thyroid function, called "TSH," instead of checking out the whole system. Other errors include over-simplified thyroid hormone replacement, usually with just one hormone, and following this intervention by just checking one or two levels. Bad treatment of thyroid dysfunction can rob you of your life, energy, and health, and in certain cases can end up costing you your thyroid gland, resulting in your having to pop a thyroid pill every day for the rest of your life.
- **Obstructive sleep apnea:** This little jewel I encountered first in my psychiatric residency, and then later when I served as the medical director of the Sleep Diagnostic Center of Indiana. Typically, but not always, this is a condition signaled by loud and obnoxious snoring and ominous stop-breathing episodes during sleep. The afflicted sufferer is usually the last to know. A gradual draining of one's energy and mental faculties, a slow rise in blood pressure, and death by heart attacks, strokes, or traffic wrecks (because of going to sleep at the wheel of a car)

are the outcomes. This condition will rob you of your career, then kill you. Do not treat it lightly.

- **The two "easy" cancers:** This one is "good news, bad news." Both of these are incredibly easy to diagnose and treat when caught early. Both will typically kill you if caught late. They are cervical cancer in women and prostate cancer in men. Both require examination in your private areas. For men, the American Cancer Society recommends digital rectal examination and a blood test, called the PSA, yearly if you are over fifty. Women don't get a "pass" until fifty, however. Recommendations are usually for pelvic exams and Pap smears once a year from adulthood on, or when sexual activity commences. Tragically, "between 60% and 80% of American women with newly diagnosed invasive cervical cancer have not had a Pap smear in the past 5 years, and many of these women have never had a Pap test," according to the American Cancer Society.
- **Obesity and smoking:** I don't differentiate between these either in terms of addictive potential, the possibility of wrecking your health and killing you, or how innocently people can slip into them. Frequently you need professional help in dealing with either one (or both) of them. Please get it. [See web resources for details.]

BIOLOGY: The "Graduate Program"

Functional Medicine and Age Management Medicine

Functional medicine may be thought of as the analysis and stabilization of the human physiological "platform" for optimum, and not just adequate, functioning. The field is broad and deep; it is also solidly supported by peer-reviewed medical literature. Many people don't take advantage of this state-of-the-art care because their own medical practitioners do not know about it . . . and most patients don't know to ask.

There are two ways to look at "Age Management Medicine." One way is conventional medical practice, an approach which is so familiar and orthodox that average practitioners at any AMA meeting would be very comfortable with it. This includes "watching your cholesterol," "controlling your weight," "exercise," and the like.

In addition to the more typical orthodox and physiological functional medicine approaches, the way that I look at age management medicine is not just the treatment of medical and psychiatric illness, but also the aggressive prosecution of a relentlessly positive physiological agenda. In addition to evaluating for both male and female hormone imbalances, there are other values which should be investigated as well. Most people, and even male chauvinist pigs in recovery, know about menopause. What most people (and many doctors) either don't know or aren't sufficiently aware of is that there are two critical sex hormones in women (both of which can go down), and, of course, one critical sex hormone in men which can go down *early* — sometimes as early as a man's forties! Indeed, men can hit "andropause" before women hit "menopause." I truly knew that age management medicine was about to "go mainstream" when I saw a cover article on low testosterone in males in one of my conventional psychiatric journals.

Using the diagnostic and therapeutic tools of functional medicine and age management medicine, people's energy levels and enthusiasm can frequently be restored to what they were in one's thirties. Imagine what you could do with that kind of energy!

Concluding Formulations

Lao Tse, the great Chinese philosopher and founder of Taoism, observed: "The new life created by the final integration is self-aware yet without ego, capable of inhabiting a body yet not attached to it, and guided by wisdom rather than emotion. Whole and virtuous, it can never die."

In this chapter, I haven't offered you the path to physical immortality, but I have offered a path to integration: of self-awareness and of ideas about how you can be "guided by wisdom rather than emotion." Emotions are fine —as long as they are occurring because of your pleasure at your own efforts. They are not fine when they result from knee jerk, automatic, unconsidered responses to stresses in your environment.

Stay well. Insure that you get the medical screening tests you need to hang on to your life. Consider dedicating a small portion of your efforts to achieving maximum performance out of your physical being. Monitor your thoughts carefully for self-deception, and your behavior for supporting your maximal efforts.

If you do, truly you will have achieved the desired end of **Working Smarter: Not Harder**, and will lead a life of achievement, emotional wellness, and maximum accomplishment.

Additional web-linked information to supplement this chapter is available at: www.drcady.com/withoutyourhead.

ABOUT LOUIS B. CADY, M.D.

Dr. Louis Cady, M.D., practices child, adolescent, adult, and forensic psychiatry in Evansville, Indiana. After obtaining his medical degree in 1989, he trained in psychiatry at the Mayo Clinic. In addition to his conventional training in medicine and psychiatry at the Mayo Clinic, Dr. Cady has subsequently received additional training in Age Management Medicine from the Cenegenics Medical Institute in Las Vegas, Nevada, and added those modalities to his practice.

He has a diverse background as a musician and as an entrepreneur. Dr. Cady has combined his life experiences in business and medicine to acquire cutting-edge marketing and positioning skills, making his independent practice of psychiatry a remarkable success in an era of managed care. In addition to his professional practice of psychiatry, Dr. Cady has become a monthly columnist, author or contributing author of three books, and a sought-after speaker, lecturer, and consultant. A member of the National Speakers Association, *Dr. Cady travels widely as a presenter for four international pharmaceutical companies and has served as an adviser, speaker, motivator, and consultant to many more area and regional businesses.*

Contact information:
Louis B. Cady, M.D.
611 Harriet Street, Suite 304
Doctors Plaza
Evansville, IN 47710
Phone: (812) 429-0772
Fax: (812) 429-0793
E-mail: LCady@DrCady.com
Website: www.DrCady.com

YES YOU CAN: *The Seven Essential Time Management Tips*

by Valerie Bernard

Some of the most important skills I have learned in life were not taught in school. Life usually hands you the lessons you need. Sometimes these lessons come in the form of personal and emotional crises. For me, they also came in the form of organizational crises.

Throughout this chapter, as you read my story, as well as those of others, I believe you will come to realize that anything is possible with persistence, the right attitude, and a few time management tips. When you find yourself in a situation with little or no hope, it is easy to give up. For me, some of the tips and quotes which follow were, and still are, roadmaps, helping me accomplish the things that I once thought were impossible.

Each section that follows will outline time management themes which enabled me to lose my fear of failure and risk doing something that was very important for me. The tips are not the only time management tips out there; however, these put me on the fast track. The quotes or stories that follow philosophies some of the ways people stay committed and, despite obstacles, manage to get so much accomplished each day.

As you read this chapter, decide whether or not the Time Management Tip (TMT) will work for you. Ask yourself how you might modify the TMT to fit your lifestyle. Discard what does not work for you and keep what does. Most importantly, you should know that I was not always organized.

My background is very simple. I grew up in a small West Virginia town. I was a graduate of the local high school; my training also included vocational education. I worked as an administrative assistant for several years until landing a job with a West Virginia Fortune 500 company. I married and had a beautiful daughter named Darby.

Ten years ago I hit a brick wall. I had a job that was literally making me sick. I was pregnant and my marriage was in trouble. After my divorce, I was a single parent with a three-month-old baby, and I was miles away from my family. At this time in my life, I felt I had hit the bottom of the barrel, as they say. The easy way out was to feel sorry for myself and to blame everyone else.

As time passed, I became a single parent, with a toddler. I still remember those nights of staying up prepping sales accounts after my daughter went to bed. This was no longer the time in my life when I could spend countless hours on the phone talking with friends or better yet, sit all evening watching my favorite shows, which I had taped from the week before. On one particular evening after Darby was sound asleep, I found myself picking up the clutter of toys that were piled atop one another in the family room. The last book I picked up was the *Little Engine that Could*. You know the book. "I think I can, I think I can." This was just the motivation I needed.

After several successful years in yellow-page sales, I was finally considering leaving my job. Yes, I was making six figures, but I was not doing what I had always wanted to do. I still remember the look on my parents' faces when I told them of my passion to leave sales and go into teaching. My parents, along with my closest friends, thought I was in need of psychiatric evaluation. In any event, with a leap of faith, I did just that. I made the decision to leave my full-time job with benefits to go to college for the first time to get a degree. The journey of future success would thus require a reorganization of how I spent my time.

My first day on campus was intimidating, to say the least. After stumbling around the campus for what seemed liked hours, I found my way first to the campus library. I discovered a whole new world in the motivational/business section. I started reading books on goal-setting, positive thinking, attitude, and psychology. At this time, I started collecting quotes that inspired me and really made me stop and think. Some of the quotes gave me inspiration and a whole new attitude. Without realizing what was happening, I was getting some answers as to why some people are more successful than others. I also realized that other people have more serious challenges than I do, yet they remain positive. Through my next several years of reading and research, I began to discover some of the tips, tools, and secrets that made these people successful.

One of the most important things I learned in the first year of being a (what they called) a non-traditional student and a single parent is that we all face challenges. How we react to them is what matters most. Learning to focus your energy on the solutions will help you accept challenges as an opportunity to learn.

To control your time, you need a very clear understanding of what is important. The following tips helped me focus on a new way of living. I discovered that many people are wandering around aimlessly, while others can organize any situation.

I have learned that success is to be measured not so much by the position that one has reached in life as by the obstacles which he has overcome while trying to succeed.

— Booker T. Washington

TMT #1

Make a Decision

Do you have a choice? Yes!

There are many choices and decisions to make in life. Sometimes they are easy and other times they are difficult. You may even hear people say that they do not have a choice. "I have no choice but to go to this conference." "I have no choice but to travel so much." Do these statements really mean that we don't have a choice, or that the choice or decision is difficult?

Thinking that you do not have a choice can lead to a life that is out of control. Sound familiar? Let's think about a few questions that can guide us in our decision-making.

- What is the issue or problem that needs to be addressed?
- What options for decisions do you realistically have?
- What is the most appropriate decision to fit the situation?
- What is the upside? The downside?
- Have you thought it through?
- Do I feel passionate about the choice I made?
- How does my decision affect everyone involved?

We all struggle at times with making decisions. The decisions I have made in my life using the "Have, Do, Be" mentality have caused me many challenges. For example, if only I had a job making $150,000 a year, I could travel more with my daughter, and this would mean I would be a great mom. I then asked myself, what might happen if I have this job and I am still not happy? Day-in and day-out I ended up in a state of worry and stress. Once I changed my thinking to "Be, Do, Have," I found my stress and worry were not as great. In other words, I will be a great mom, and do things with my daughter, and have wonderful memories. I do not need the $150,000 a year job to be a great mom. Try making decisions not based on what you will get as a result, and, by doing so, you will make a choice — a wise one.

Story: "The Three Frogs"

Question: Three frogs sat on a log and one decided to jump off. How many frogs were left on the log?

Answer: Three

Explanation: Although almost everyone answers "two," the correct answer is "three."

Just because the frog *decided* to jump off the log does not necessarily mean that he actually *did.*

Is there a gap between what you decide to do and what you actually do?

Once I began the rigorous schedule of student and mom, I began to realize I was not only financially poor, but also time poor. I still remember sitting in the library at the university wondering if my decision to leave my job to go to college was the right one. This was definitely a dramatic change. At the point when I left full-time employment to be a full-time college student and full-time mother, I knew exactly what I wanted to accomplish. The decision had been made; look forward not back. I wanted to be a trainer, a teacher, and a coach. More important I wanted to be a catalyst for change in people's lives, strengthening self-confidence and sparking higher goals in learning, work, and life.

As I walked across campus the next several weeks, I was completely lost. I had lost sight of my original plan, my original goal. While I was sitting on a bench perusing my schedule wondering which way I needed to go next, a college professor stopped by to chat. I commented on my lack of direction, my confusion, and my frustration. This particular professor became one of my greatest cheerleaders over the next several years. I still remember her response to my question of which direction to head. She said, "It depends on where you want to go." She reminded me that the whole reason why I was on this campus was to get an education and to prepare myself for teaching and training. Before my next class, sitting right on that very bench, I began to think about what had made me a top performer in my previous job. It became very clear to me that I had always developed very clear goals and objectives. I had always had a strong belief in goal-setting. Throughout my life, goals have kept me focused (and so did Dr. Wyant).

TMT #2

Define Your Goals

Goals Work!

In order to begin the goal-setting process, you must ask yourself a few questions:

- What do you want to achieve?
- Are your goals crystal clear?
- Are your goals practical and obtainable?
- Have you defined both short-term and long-term goals?
    - 1-2 years (Short term)
    - 5-10 years (Long term)
- What action do I need to take right now to achieve my goals?

Have you written down your answers? Have you given your goal a timeframe? (Sometimes the yellow sticky notes are everywhere, e.g., bathroom mirror, steering wheel, computer monitor.) In any event, write them down.

Taking action sometimes means developing new skills or acquiring additional knowledge and information. Don't forget to review your goals from time to time. Also consider charting your progress in order to see the light at the end of the tunnel.

Story:

"Would you tell me which way I ought to go from here?," asked Alice.

"That depends a good deal on where you want to get," said the Cat.

"I really don't care where," replied Alice.

"Then it really doesn't matter which way you go," said the Cat.

— Lewis Carroll, novelist and poet (1832-1898), *Alice's Adventures in Wonderland* (1865).

The next morning and several mornings thereafter, the alarm would ring at 6:00 a.m. I might mention that it was not a soothing ring. I would invariably reset the alarm and drift back to sleep. What had happened? I had always worked out, showered, and dressed by the time my daughter, Darby, woke from her sleep. The situation was a little different now. "Snooze" had become my middle name. I spent most mornings running around my cluttered house trying to find what I needed for class. Everyday was the same . . . homework, classes, and parenting (and wishing for an extra hour each day, and an extra day each week).

Remember that professor I mentioned earlier? Well, she brought me a book just in the nick of time. In *How to Think and Act Like a Chief Executive*, C. Ray Johnson states: "Prioritizing is the answer to time management problems . . . not computers, efficiency experts, or matrix scheduling. You do not need to do work faster or to eliminate gaps in productivity to make better use of your time. You need to spend more time on the right things. . . ." WOW! On that same bench at the university campus, I thought about this time management tip. How could I prioritize and plan ahead in order to make maximum use of my time? That evening I decided to plan my next day. Yes, indeed, it was the night before. I made my list of goals for the next day so I would be ready to go when the alarm rang the next morning.

TMT #3

Plan & Prioritize

The basis of time management is planning and prioritizing. If you plan the night before, it will be more likely that you will accomplish your goals the next day. We all have so much to do. It seems we never have enough time to get the things done we want to accomplish. And if the time becomes available, where is our energy? Planning ahead and prioritizing will allow you to have more of both: time and energy.

In TMT #2 we defined our goals. Planning requires developing a set of action steps to achieve our goals. If we plan and prioritize effectively, then we can eliminate time wasters and get closer to our destination. Consider the 80/20 rule: For unstructured activities, (or our typical activities) 80 percent of the effort gives less than 20 percent of the valuable outcome (or value of our work). In other words, you either spend much time on deciding what to do next, or you are taking many unnecessary, unfocused, and inefficient steps.

Now ask yourself these questions:

- Have you completed your "To Do" list?
- Have you prioritized your "To Do" list?

Now the semester was in full swing. Each student's schedule reflected unique priorities and responsibilities . . . mine was no different. I began to wonder if my relationship with time was a happy one. I came to realize through conversations with my classmates, most of whom were at least 10 years younger than I, that certain times of the day were more productive. This time of the day for me was in the evening from 8:00 p.m. when my daughter went to bed until 2:00 a.m. when I would begin to look cross-eyed at the computer screen.

Once I began scheduling my priorities during my personal "prime-time," I began to accomplish more with less time. When I began to plan on paper, I was ready to meet the challenges ahead. Planning on paper stimulates creativity and allows you to adjust schedules and commitments accordingly.

TMT #4

Identify your "prime-time"

Keep track of your energy levels!

By identifying your "prime-time," i.e., when you have the most energy, you are well on your way. Planning on paper enables you to see yourself in a new way. Once you have prioritized your activities, including the time-frames for completion, your journey to success is well under way.

- Have you developed a list including all activities, priorities, and estimated completion times?

Activities	Priorities	Completion Time	Best Time To Do

1. To fill in the table above, list all your daily activities and current projects.
2. Rank your activities in the priorities column in order of importance (truly important).
3. Give yourself a timeframe to finish the activity in the "completion time" column.
4. Determine what time of the day you work best, i.e., morning, afternoon, or evening, and schedule the most difficult activities during this time.

Check off the activities and projects as you complete them. If you forget to put something on your activities table that you completed, then by all means reward yourself and add it to the list . . . checking it off makes you feel better!!

- Have you developed a daily, weekly, monthly plan?

	Monday	Tuesday	Wednesday	Thursday	Friday
6 a.m.					
7 a.m.					
8 a.m.					
9 a.m.					
10 a.m.					
11 a.m.					
12 p.m.					
1 p.m.					
2 p.m.					
3 p.m.					
4 p.m.					
5 p.m.					

Planners, organizers, calendars, palm pilots, handhelds, PDA's . . . how do you choose? No matter what you choose, it is important to have one single, solitary place to record your activities and appointments. Remember all those sticky notes . . . time to get rid of them by logging them into your planner.

- Have you identified your top priority tasks?
- Can anything be delegated?
- How can you plan in order to avoid obstacles or delays?

Do you schedule appointments after lunch when you already have an 11:00 a.m. appointment? What if the 11:00 appointment runs long?

"To choose time is to save time."

— Frances Bacon

I was well on my way to finishing my bachelor degree and was making plans to pursue my master's degree. I had also defined my goals in writing for completing the degree program. The timeframe had been established and I had begun to plan, on paper of course. The next task before me was to conquer the clutter. My home office was the epitome of chaos, as papers, tests, and projects were stacked everywhere. What was next for me? GET ORGANIZED!

It is possible to be successful and disorganized. It is just a little bit more difficult if you think this way. Believe me; I know. You should have seen my desk, not to mention how much precious time I wasted because I was swimming in clutter. It was definitely time to turn my mess into success.

TMT #5

Reorganize your office or work area

A well-organized office or work area helps you locate information and documents quickly. A tremendous amount of time is wasted when you have to search for documents. When you are surrounded by clutter, you tend to feel overwhelmed and distracted. Is your desk or work area completely clear with the exception of the project you are currently working on?

- Is your work-area organized?

There are four basic things you can do to get your work area organized:

- Handle It
- File It
- Delegate It
- Get Rid of It

Surveys show that average Americans spend an entire year of their working lives searching through desk clutter or looking for misplaced objects. Executives waste up to six weeks a year looking for misfiled papers. Are you overwhelmed by paper? Are you overwhelmed by too little time?

Organization is critical to success and high performance. Remember to look closely at your goals when trying to become more organized. Removing obstacles that do not permit easy access to completing your daily activities can be of great benefit to you. The general rule of thumb is, if the item is not essential to your current list of activities or if you have not used something in a year, pitch it.

One of the hardest things for me to learn was how to say "no." It seemed that everyone always had requests. Realizing you have only 24 hours in each day and only seven days in each week will help you manage your time more wisely. As you become a better time manager, invariably you will get more requested of you. So the next time someone asks you if you have a minute, your answer will be "______". That is right! No. Stick to it!

TMT #6

Just say no

Are you the one who is known for always pitching in? Are you the one who keeps at it long after normal working hours? Or have you just gotten in the habit of working until seven or eight o'clock? Have I got the answer for you . . . just say no. If this seems too harsh, practice saying, "Let me think about it and I will get back to you."

If you are uncomfortable about saying no, suggest some other alternatives to the person making the request. Dr. Donald Wetmore, author of B*eat the Clock,* suggests trying these strategies.

- "I'm sorry. That is not a priority for me right now."
- "I can't help you on this now, but I can get it next week. Would that be okay?"
- "I have so much on my plate now; I don't know when I can get to it. But I do know someone who can help you now."
- "Before I take this on for you, let me show you a few things so that you might be able to do it yourself."

- "I have made so many commitments to others; it would be unfair to them and you if I took on anything more at this point."

And as you speak, smile.

It is 10:00 p.m. and Darby is screaming because she has an ear infection. In the kitchen the dishes are piled to the ceiling. I can't even walk in what we call the laundry room, and I have comprehensive exams the very next day, which will finish up my master's degree. Are you starting to get the picture? As frightening as this may sound, it is a fact of life for any parent trying to go to school. You can balance family and college. I did it and so can you!

In Stephen Covey's *The Seven Habits of Highly Effective People*, Covey tells us to "sharpen your saw." Covey asks you to imagine meeting someone in the woods working feverishly to saw down a tree.

"You look exhausted," you exclaim. "How long have you been at it?"

"Over five hours," he returns, "and I'm beat! This is hard work."

"Well, why don't you take a break for a few minutes and sharpen that saw?" Emphatically, the man answers, "I'm too busy sawing!"

To be the most effective parent, student, friend, or time manager, you will need to recharge your battery. A balanced lifestyle includes many activities: physical, intellectual, social, career, emotional, and spiritual. Setting time aside for all these activities will give you a better perspective.

TMT #7

Recharge Your Battery

The best plans fail because we forget this important tip. When planning your schedule, (TMT # 4), don't forget to schedule time for family, friends, and special projects. It seems we all assign the "whatever time is left" to these activities. Balance is the key to recharging your battery. Look at recharging your battery as a wise investment.

"Never give up! Never, never, never, never, never give up!"

— Winston Churchill

Conclusion

Life is an event that is continually evolving. I continue to modify my goals as I reach different stages of success. After I earned a master's degree in adult education, I began my entrepreneurial dream and started my own training company, Executive Training Centers, Inc. (ETC). When times are hard, I try not to lose sight of my goals of continually improving personal performance. Time Management is one of those goals. Poor time management makes for a poor salesperson, a poor parent, a poor team-player. By managing time, you can reduce stress and anxiety.

Time is so valuable. Time management can help you be more productive and successful. Along the way, don't forget to schedule some time for you.

Story: Rocks in a Jar

One day an expert in time management was speaking to a group of business students and, to drive home a point, used an illustration those students will never forget.

As she stood in front of the group of high-powered overachievers she said, "Okay, time for a quiz." Then she pulled out a one-gallon, wide mouthed Mason jar and set it on the table in front of the students. She then produced about a dozen fist-sized rocks and carefully placed them, one at a time, into the jar.

When the jar was filled to the top and no more rocks would fit inside, she asked, "Is this jar full?" Everyone in the class said, "Yes." Then she said, "Really?" She reached under the table and pulled out a bucket of gravel. Then she dumped some gravel in and shook the jar, causing pieces of gravel to work themselves down into the space between the big rocks.

Then she asked the group once more, "Is the jar full?" By this time the class was on to her. "Probably not," one of them answered. "Good," she replied. She reached under the table and brought out a bucket of sand. She started dumping the sand in the jar, which went into all of the spaces left between the rocks and the gravel.

Once more she asked the question, "Is this jar full?" "No!," the class shouted. Once again she said, "Good." Then she grabbed a pitcher of water and began to pour it in until the jar was filled to the brim.

Then she looked at the class and asked, "What is the point of this illustration?"

One eager beaver raised his hand and said, "The point is, no matter how full your schedule is, if you try really hard you can always fit some more things in it!"

"No," the speaker replied, "that is not the point. The truth this illustration teaches us is: If you don't put the big rocks in first, you'll never get them in at all."

What are the big rocks in your life? Your children . . . Your loved ones . . . Your education . . . Your dreams . . . Teaching or mentoring others . . . Doing the things that you love . . . Time for yourself . . . Your health . . .

Remember to put these BIG ROCKS in first or you'll never get them in at all.

Summary

- Make A Decision
- Define Your Goals
- Plan & Prioritize
- Identify Your Prime-Time
- Reorganize Your Office or Work Area
- Just Say No
- Recharge Your Battery

FYI

My wonderful inspiration and awesome daughter, Darby, is 9 years old now. My loving and supportive parents, Van and Betty Bernard, are thankful I followed my dream. (I can't wait to tell them I am enrolling in a Ph.D. program.) My mentor and friend, Dr. Laura Wyant, is still laughing about my ability to get all the rocks in the jar. Last but not least, this chapter is dedicated to my hero, Chet Marshall, who helps illuminate my path with his never-ending encouragement and support.

ABOUT VALERIE BERNARD

High-energy, entertaining, and educational are words used to describe Valerie Bernard's presentations. Her combination of expertise, humor, and inspiration energizes people to take action in both their personal and business lives.

Valerie's dedication and commitment are demonstrated by her ability to take care of her daughter while working and attending graduate school. As a single mother she went on to an award-winning sales and sales management career. In addition to her sales, management, and educational background, Valerie was the Director of Dale Carnegie Training. It was through this position that Valerie discovered her own entrepreneurial spirit and founded Executive Training Centers, Inc. In addition, Valerie is an Adjunct Professor of Adult Education at Marshall University. She has conducted over 300 training and development workshops. Valerie's own life story proves that you can rise above any challenge and accomplish your dreams. With her own personal stories, Valerie teaches others the Seven Simple Time Management Technique's (TMT's) that took her from having no money to a life of personal and financial independence. Ms. Bernard is recognized as an Independent Certified Facilitator with The Greatest Salesman, Inc., and is qualified to administer and interpret the Hartman Value Profile. She is also certified to administer the Myers-Briggs Type Indicator (MBTI) that is distributed by Consulting Psychologists Press (CPP). Executive Training Centers, Inc., specializes in consulting, keynote presentations, retreats, meeting facilitation, coaching and training services.

Contact Information:

Valerie Bernard
Executive Training Centers, Inc.
2808 Birch Avenue
Point Pleasant, WV 25550
Phone: (304) 593-2401
E-mail: etcwv@charter.net
Website: www.etcwv.com
and www.ogmandino.com/etcwv

T.I.M.E. Test Your Way Towards Achievement

by Debra Kimbrough

You've probably had some good ideas over the years. No, they were great ideas. But while you were getting ready to get ready, other folks around our planet thought of and implemented your ideas. "Hey, that was my idea! I thought of it first." — you said out loud to anyone who would listen. In gift-giving it may be the thought that counts, but that's simply not true when talking about accomplishing our dreams. Accomplishments require more than the thoughts derived from the conjuring up of ideas. Seeing a dream through to fruition is the result of selecting an idea for which you can sustain a passion, identifying your available resources, developing a plan of action, and then taking consistent action on that plan. The result being that you are working smarter, rather than harder.

Throughout my life, I've had a burning desire to make a positive difference in children's lives. However, there was a weekend years ago when I entertained the idea of another passion. Working as a child care abuse and neglect investigator, I found that crocheting was a great stress reducer. Of course depending on my stress level, I'd end up with either a loosely woven afghan, or a tightly spun potholder.

Crocheting a tea pot one Friday night, I noticed that the handle was taking the shape of my dog's ear. Thrilled beyond belief, I ran to my yarn basket and retrieved one grey skein and one pink. With growing excitement, stitches were added and dropped until my fifteen year old Chihuahua, Duke, had some pretty snazzy bunny ears. Well, that's all it took. Crocheting the entire night, I ended up with an entire millinery of six different pet party hats. That's it! Brian Tracy says never stop looking for it. I'd found it! — My big idea. Or, at least, I thought so. Pet Party Hats — to be the first edition of my pet periodical entitled *Party Animals*. It was bound to be a success.

At sunrise I rushed Duke and his new headgear to a nearby store that had a photo booth in the foyer — curtain and all. My four-legged model squirmed as his hats were switched between each flash. Hence, countless quarters were spent to get the six headshots. It took that many because with every other flash I had to bend over to pick up my not-so-cooperative model and his hats. It would certainly have been more efficient to shoot all bunny ears, then pumpkin hats, and so on. By the time I got home I was not only suffering from sleep deprivation, but my enthusiasm for my never-to-be-published pet periodical had dwindled down to the thought of, "WHAT WAS I THINKING?"

Why did this great idea not work? Because I did not sustain and feed my passion for my project, nor did I establish and follow a plan of action. These steps would have resulted in my working smarter. Instead, I was thinking and working harder. Further self-evaluation of this earlier unmet goal reveals that available resources were not accessed. I could have hired others who enjoyed crocheting and probably would have appreciated the piece-work that they could have completed in the comfort of their own homes. Authoring the hat patterns and providing each to my dedicated, crochet-loving, contract workers would have left me free to locate crochet magazine editors who were seeking patterns to publish and to contact consignment stores that would sell the finished products. Think of the potential sponsors — veterinarians, large pet supply stores, and yarn companies. But it was not to be. I tucked the idea away in a yarn box.

Looking back over my ten years as a full-time professional speaker and child care consultant, what have I done to ensure working smarter, not harder? It's definitely been an evolution. My general recipe for working smarter, not harder, helps me to focus on what is important. In recent years, my use of this recipe resulted in my accomplishing more, in less time, and with less effort, than I did in earlier years. Apply the following T.I.M.E. Test to develop and improve your own personal plan of action.

Time — Be honest with yourself as to how you spend your time. An epidemic in many homes and businesses is the presence of folks complaining about how much work they have to do. Yet you see them visiting, taking long breaks, and lengthy lunches. When it's time to leave for the day, they dart out the door. Or, perhaps they have to stay later to accomplish the tasks that could have been knocked out earlier, with less visiting. If phone calls and interruptions rule your day and you never get back to your intended tasks, take charge of your time. You will find blocks of time available to spend towards achieving your dreams.

Inspiration — Inspiration results in increased passion. And, when you have passion, you have the makings to achieve your dreams. Stay focused on the possibilities. Live, eat, breathe, and feed yourself positive thoughts. That means you must surround yourself with inspiring people. Instead of watching a television trauma drama, select an uplifting, encouraging story. Read any and all books written by the greats: Norman Vincent Peale and Og Mandino are two of my all-time favorites. Add to your list Denis Waitley's book, *Timing Is Everything*. Another terrific book that will help those of you who are plagued with the heel-dragging syndrome is Rita Emmett's book, *The Procrastinator's Handbook*. Also, carry motivational audio tapes/cd's in your car. Zig Ziglar and Ken

Blanchard don't know it, but they've traveled across Texas with me many times. Feed the inspiration you gain from these works by beginning to create your plan of action. Reading and listening to these inspirational leaders, I gained the courage and confidence to step out on faith and follow my dreams. You can too! What's your passion? Feed it daily!

Money — Let's face it. Money management (or not) is the undoing of many a would-be entrepreneur. Take charge of your finances. Get advice if need be. Identify the amount of money you have available and the amount of money you will need to help you achieve your dreams. One thing I knew before leaving my full-time job with the state of Texas was that I did not have a clue as to how much money I would make. So I spent two years while still employed eliminating as much debt as possible. This reduced the amount I'd need when I went out on my own. Who knew when I took the plunge that I'd face some incredible obstacles? The first ten months on my own, I had no vehicle and had to depend on the city bus to get me from presentation to presentation. While it was an humbling experience, I still felt successful. My enthusiasm did not wane. And since I was doing what I loved to do, most of the time it did not seem like work. Your state of mind is a crucial factor in how you regard your financial highs and lows. Make the most of your money resources and you will definitely be working smarter.

Efforts — Understanding that increased effort equals increased results, identify those persons who possess the skills necessary to help you achieve your dreams. For the longest time, being little Ms. Independent, I thought I had to do everything myself or it didn't count. Thank goodness I've gotten off of that high-horse. Accepting what you're good at, and farming out the rest, will result in accomplishing more in less time. Of course, if you're good at everything you'll have to pry yourself away. (That doesn't happen to be one of my problems.) Otherwise, you're back to working harder, not smarter.

Unfortunately, I've witnessed people give up their passion that they gave a heck of a lot more thought and planning to than I gave to my pet party hats. Maybe it wasn't their true passion either. I hope that they did not quit without first considering that it may not have been that their idea was an impossible achievement, but rather, they lacked an effective plan of action and T.I.M.E. Test. Their dreams seemed too difficult to attain, so they gave up before ever really getting started. I nearly did that myself.

Barely out of the starting gate into self-employment, I convinced myself that I didn't like cold calls to the point that I became immobilized. "Forget this noise!" I told myself. "This is too hard." I called my boss back at the state agency where I'd left only three months before. She enthusiastically accepted my call and plea to get my old job back. It was a done deal. I'd start back on Monday and even have my same caseload as before.

As I lowered the receiver, I experienced a bizarre inner struggle. My sense of relief at returning to the security of a paycheck with paid benefits was being drowned out by a sense of failure and shame. I immediately realized that these negative feelings were the result of giving up on my dream to help parents, teachers, and caregivers protect children by teaching them better guidance skills. My passion for my dream being stronger than my fear and desire for a steady paycheck, it took me only a few minutes to call her back. I'm sure she thought that I'd lost my marbles. But I didn't care. What I did care about was not having regrets. I vowed to give it my all. The funny thing is that by giving it my all, I ended up enjoying cold calls.

As you can see from my recipe, it all comes down to T.I.M.E. Without a doubt T.I.M.E. represents our most valuable resources. If we are to work smarter, not harder, we must harness and make the most of our Time, Inspiration, Money and Efforts.

To bring you up to date, my current canine friend is Bogie. And while he has no experience modeling, he does get to wear the pet party hats. My favorite is the pumpkin hat. You see, you may have to bury the dog, but you can always recycle the hats.

ABOUT DEBRA KIMBROUGH

Debra Kimbrough helps adults better protect children by improving their child guidance and supervision skills. Debra started A Better Caregiver Workshops *(ABC), a child-care training company, in 1994, specializing in the supervision and guidance of children. Since 1989, she's presented over 1500 seminars at educational and faith-based conferences. Author of* Octavia's New Red Shoes, Forty Days To Good Guidance: A Handbook For Adults Working With Young Children *and numerous child-care related articles, she is also the singer and songwriter of four music tapes. As an expert witness, Debra uses her previous experience of abuse/neglect investigations and the licensing of child care facilities, having testified in over 100 child-care related injury cases. Debra's presentations are much sought after due to her infectious humor, interesting perspective and unique way of helping others remember what they learn. A member of the National Speaker's Association since 1997 and numerous industry-related associations, Debra's gift to her attendees is to help them* Take A Light-Hearted Look At Serious Subjects.

Contact Information:
Debra Kimbrough
P.O. Box 1539
Kemah, TX 77565
Phone: (281) 339-4507
E-mail: debra@debrakimbrough.com
Website: DebraKimbrough.com

Buy the Farm and Live to Tell About It

by Cynthia Mustaine Hettinger

When I was young, I dreamed of living on a farm. Most people dream of living in a big city, but I had done that. What I truly wanted was a house in the country surrounded by land and animals. I reached that goal only when I learned self-empowerment through personal responsibility. The ironic part was that, once I had the farm, I was so busy juggling the various roles I played in life that everything was out of balance and stressful. It is through experience that we learn the most life-changing lessons. Through the years, I have learned that I can have my farm (my dream) and enjoy the process (integrating my roles in life). I knew how to work hard, but experience has taught me how to work smart.

Self Empowerment

Obstacles

We create obstacles in our lives that de-power who we are and what we can achieve. The first key to releasing your inner resources and empowering yourself is to recognize the obstacles you set. I cannot state enough how this is something you do to yourself. It is self-sabotage. Only you can give your power to someone else. Know from the core of your being that you and only you are responsible for your life. You are able to respond, to make choices. You have the power to make your life great. Many of us use all that power to make our life not so great.

Some obstacles that we commonly place in our way:

1. **Blame** — We blame the circumstances of our lives on other people or situations. A common story is "my father/mother was an alcoholic" or "I come from a dysfunctional family." I know more adult children of alcoholics than I know adult children of non-alcoholics. And yes, growing up in an abusing alcoholic family definitely affects our behavior. However, as an adult, that excuse is a self created obstacle. There are so many of us adult children of alcoholics that we have created wonderful methods for working through that pain and learning new behavior patterns. The resources for getting help are unlimited, so using the excuse of "being an adult child" is creating an obstacle. Turning that truth into a positive process of learning new behavior is available. Blame comes from a position of non-growth. Everyone has a story. Some people have many stories. Some stories are happening to you today. The difference between creating an obstacle and creating self-power is your choice. The choice of blame creates an obstacle. The choice of learning creates power.
2. **Dishonesty** — We love to hide the truth from the person who knows us best — ourselves. Learning to be honest with ourselves is tough. We get caught in making things up that make us comfortable. My education on this occurred when my brother came to visit us from South Africa. He had not been home for over 10 years. I was looking forward to his visit, but when he arrived I found him hard to be with. He was very bossy. He spent most of our time together telling me how I should do things. It drove me crazy. One morning my husband asked me why I was not spending much time with my brother. I explained that it was because my brother was so bossy that I found myself angry with him. My dear husband just laughed and said,

"Honey, you are just like your brother." I was baffled and said "I am not." My husband's reply was, "Actually you are. You, your sister and brother are the bossiest people I have ever been around." I thought about this for a minute and asked, "How can you love me?" He said one of the many reasons he loved me was that I had a kind heart. Thank goodness for my wonderful husband. But I still sat there and realized how I had not been honest with myself. I am bossy. I know why, but the "why" does not excuse the behavior. And admitting I am bossy helped me realize how that behavior harmed my relationships. Being open to my husband's loving observations and being honest with myself opened doors for me to change my behavior and improve all my relationships. So ask yourself what you are being dishonest about.

3. **Guilt** — Feelings of guilt create many obstacles that keep us from moving forward. If we have lived at all, we have said something or acted in a way that we later regret. We have hurt someone with our words or actions, we have said "yes" when a "no" would have been a better choice, or we said "no" when a "yes" would have served a better purpose. Holding on to that guilt is like planting our feet in cement. To move forward we must move out of guilt. The following exercise can help. If you have hurt someone, then simply go back to that person and say that you are sorry. It is not your responsibility if he or she does not accept the apology. You cannot control that part of the process. What you can control is your behavior. The act of sincerely apologizing releases your guilt. If the person is no longer in your life, then write a letter. Even though the person will not receive this letter, your mind doesn't know the difference between what is real and what is imagined. In your mind, the act of writing the letter of apology is an act of forgiveness. List all

the guilt that you hold in your heart. Go through the action of asking for forgiveness, and accept that forgiveness for yourself — even if it is just in your mind. Your mind is the most powerful tool you have, and your mind will create the forgiveness needed. Because I have teenage children, I am more aware of the following note of caution. Apologizing and asking for forgiveness does not give you the ticket to continue the behavior. Let go of the guilt, apologize, ask forgiveness (especially from yourself), and do not repeat the behavior. The key is in the learning. Let go of your guilt and the obstacle surrounding that guilt.

4. **Limited belief** — Our thoughts affect our beliefs; our beliefs affect our actions. Let go of those limited beliefs that say "I am too old," " I am too short," "I am not strong enough," "I can't have it all," "I am not smart enough," "This is the only way to do it," "No one can do that," "It should be this way." Stop the negative self-talk and the limited beliefs it creates. Stop the negative self-talk and replace it with positive affirmations. Instead of saying, "No one has done this before," say "I may not know anyone who has done this before; however, I will be the first person I know who has done it."

Your thought pattern, your belief system, has all the power. If you believe something cannot be done, then it will not be done. However, if you believe it can be done, then it will. An example of this truth is a cow on our farm. We have a cow name Casey who thinks she is a horse. Of course, I cannot read her thoughts, but I can read her behavior. Casey acts and behaves like a horse. She has been raised with horses and that is what she believes she is. The horses on our farm accept her as a horse. She behaves like a horse and has the life of a horse. Why? Because Casey has a belief system that does not include bovine limitations.

Dreams/Goals

The second key to self-empowerment is giving yourself permission to dream. Let yourself dream without limitations. Write down your dreams. List your dreams in all aspects of your life: career, health, family, friends, home, spiritual, education, financial and recreation.

When you write down your dreams they become goals. Goals are attainable. I have an ongoing list of dream/goals. Once I have reached a specific dream/goal, I then put a line through that item. I keep the whole list, and at this point it is many pages long. I keep this list in a special place and look at it daily. Even though my dream/goal list is in its own separate book, I relate to this list the same way as my daily "to do" list.

Do you create a daily "to do" list of things you need to accomplish? For example, a "to do" list may contain the following: go to the bank, take dog to vet, buy milk. Most of us create "to do" lists to remember the important things that need to get done. When you write your daily list, do you have any doubt in your mind about accomplishing these tasks? It never crosses your mind, right? You are writing them down to keep them in your consciousness (to remember) and to reduce stress (stress from not having milk in the refrigerator). You have every reason to believe the task will be done. And when you accomplish something on your list, you draw a line through that item. I do the same thing with my dream/goal wish list. I write down what I want, never believing that it cannot be done. Some items take years, but they get accomplished. Some items are broken down into smaller tasks, but it all gets done.

Owning a farm is on my list of dreams/goals. It has a line through it now. I wrote the dream/goal many years ago. At the time, I was a single mother living in a large city, earning just enough money to cover the basic expenses. But the farm was something I wanted, so I wrote it on my list with conviction. Create your list. Remember, you have the power to create your life. Give yourself permission to dream with conviction.

Planning the How

Now that you have written down your dreams and goals, you will be pleasantly surprised at how the universe responds to your wishes. Many things just come to pass. However, empowerment means understanding you have the responsibility to make things happen. Not all your wishes will appear like magic. Many dreams demand action on your part. In these situations, you decide the how — how to make something happen in your life. If your goal is to become a world renowned chef, then you need to take the steps toward that goal. Going to culinary school would be one way to make this happen. While planning the How, quiet the negative voice in your head, that voice that tells you, "You can't because." Every time you hear your negative voice, counteract the message with an affirmation. If your wish is to become a chef and you need to go to culinary school, stop the negative voice that says you can't go to culinary school because you have to work full time to support the family now. Quiet the voice with an affirmation and then plan the How. Plan how to go to school and work full time. Your options may include going to school part-time on Saturdays or evenings or asking your boss for a flex schedule so you can attend one morning class a week. Nothing is impossible; it is just a matter of how creative you want to be in discovering the How.

Many of the hows that my husband and I are constantly creating involve managing a successful livestock farm. When we decided to turn our farmland into a successful livestock operation, we had only the dream. We visualized what we wanted and created the How. Many new farms (like many businesses) fail. Most successful family farms are second and third generation. Two city folks moving to the country to develop a successful livestock farm did not paint a picture of success. However, we always saw success. And we figured out the How. We read many books and magazine articles on farming. We consulted with many farmers. We asked many questions. We honestly reviewed our strengths and weaknesses. My husband is better at growing hay, building fences and repairing farm equipment. I am better at caring for the animals, strategic business plans, marketing and sales. We learned by trial and error and we never gave up. I believe all these factors contributed to our success. However, there was one key factor. We behaved as if we were already successful. Both sets of our parents were raised on farms; our grandparents were very successful farmers. The problem was that our grandparents and our parents had passed away. We had only our memory of them to idealize how our successful grandparents had farmed. But that did not stop us. Whenever we came upon a challenge we would ask, "How would our grandparents have handled this?" And the answer to that was how we behaved. The How was not difficult because we had great belief that we were already successful.

Take Action

Now jump out of your comfort zone and take action. Don't allow yourself to stay in the dreaming and planning stage. Take action and do something. Do not wait until everything is perfect. Do not wait for that special moment. You have the internal resources. Give yourself the power to move.

Getting rid of obstacles, setting dreams and goals, planning the How and taking action, empowered my husband and I to create a successful livestock farm. This is not to say that everything was easy. In fact, it was not. In two years we experienced two floods, one drought, and one major blizzard. Weather happens and in those two years we had a lot of weather. How we chose to respond made the difference in behaving as victims or behaving as persons with self-power. The choice was ours. You have choices too.

One side effect of self-empowerment is to create such a full life that you become overwhelmed. When this happened to me, I crashed. I could not function. I had empowered myself into overload. So I had to learn balance. I had to learn how to integrate all the roles in both my personal and professional life.

Integrating Your Professional and Personal Roles

There are many Amish families in the county where my family and I live. One day while grocery shopping, I noticed an Amish woman and her eight children and thought how very clear her role was. How very clear the roles were for each member of the Amish family and community. I began to envy her — until I remembered she did not have indoor plumbing. This woman whom I did not know appeared very clear in her role. If she was out of balance, it was not because her professional roles and personal roles were pulling her in different directions. She would never have a manager say to her, "I do not want to hear any of my employees tell me that they have children." I did envy her.

But I do not live in an Amish community and this is not the year of my grandmother. This is the 21st century and along with indoor plumbing, I live in a society where we are expected to perform many roles. Even though the roles are clear, how to integrate each role can be difficult.

What roles do you play in your life? Are you a spouse, parent, sibling, child, employee, employer, friend? List the number of roles you play in your life.

My list looks like this:

Personal life	**Professional life**
wife	business owner
mother	entrepreneur
sister	employer
sister-in-law	livestock farmer
daughter	animal nurse
daughter-in-law	animal trainer
aunt	marketer
niece	salesperson
cousin	book keeper

patient
customer
student (we are always learning)
cook
chauffer
cleaning lady
friend
pet owner
webmaster
nutritionist
speaker
coach
trainer
author
student
event planner

How long is your list? The business owner is not the only person who performs many roles, the employee does too. No longer are job descriptions simple. When describing a job, we include many different roles. For example, the nurse is also a counselor, a book keeper, nutritionist, teacher, and a secret code decoder (can you read the doctor's handwriting?). Even within one role, we have many small roles. No wonder we are stressed and confused.

So how do we integrate all these roles within our personal and professional lives and maintain balance, productivity, and peace of mind? The first step is to work from the whole. The next step is setting goals and priorities. Then develop a method for delegating and time blocking. And finally, enjoy the harvest.

Working from the Whole

Many of us are under the illusion that we need to separate our roles to be successful. The very act of separation creates imbalance. We can no more separate the roles we play than separate the parts of our body. Every part is of the whole. Balance requires us to focus on what role or part we are using at the time. When we write, we use our hand, eyes and brain. We do not separate our hand from our body; however, our hand is where we focus.

We are the combination of our different roles. We are always a child long after our parents have died. The child role is part of our whole being: it is part of who we are. When we behave as if we are a separate person when portraying a different role, we create internal confusion.

Remember Gregory Peck as Atticus in the classic movie, *To Kill a Mocking Bird*? When Atticus was in court, his focus was on his role as an attorney. But even in court, Atticus was Scout and Jem's father. Atticus was always very clear about who he was. One of Jem's lessons in the story was discovering who his father was and how many roles his father played. The combination of these roles formed Atticus. Atticus was Jem's father, but so much more. This fact was demonstrated so well in the scene in which Atticus shoots the rabid dog. In Jem's eyes, Atticus was "just" his father. Jem was surprised to learn his father was also the best shot in the county.

Setting Goals

We have already discussed the dream/goal wish list. Mine is actually a journal. This journal is not something I carry with me throughout the day.

I learned years ago to keep an organizer. What I learned is to use one organizer for both my professional life and my personal life. This organizer contains a calendar, appointments, annual goals list, monthly and weekly goals list, daily "to do" list, and address and contact book. I have one life and I keep myself organized using one tool. Also, it is too stressful to force myself to remember everything, so I write everything down. I write everything in its proper place and forget about it. I trust that when I need it, the information will be there.

If you believe only organized people function this way, that is not true. Smart people write everything down and use a process for organization. I am not naturally very organized. I learned to function efficiently by making myself organized. Some days this process is a struggle. However, being organized reduces stress, develops efficiency and creates time.

When you set your goals and the Hows for your life, remember you have only one life. Use one tool for organizing and keep everything in one place.

Establishing Priorities

In your organizer, list your goals in order of priority. Realize that our priorities change. Priorities change during the different stages of our life. Some roles and our goals will take a higher priority than others, depending on where we are in our life process. Also, priorities change with the different seasons and even the different days of the week. My highest priority in the spring is on the farm. Spring is when the livestock are delivering babies. It is a very busy and important time. The care and attention to the livestock and my role as animal caretaker are top priority. Then in the summer, the farm work slows down for me. The children are on summer break, and my highest priority is spending quality time with them.

When you prioritize, remember that life involves balance. There is a time for everything and everything changes. Allow yourself flexibility.

Delegating

Superman and Superwoman are comic characters. Fortunately for us, they are not real. Trying to handle every responsibility in your life is impossible. Just because you can do something does not mean it is the smartest use of your time. Choose the best places to use your energy and time. Delegate the responsibilities that are your weakness or least enjoyable items. Cleaning house is mine. I love a clean house, but I hate to clean. So I have hired a cleaning person. By delegating this responsibility to someone else, I can place my energy in the areas of my strengths and areas that I enjoy.

Many people do not delegate because they do not want to lose control. However, when you delegate, you actually gain more control. You are the one who hired someone else to do something better than you. You did not control the process, but you did control the outcome.

By delegating, you can get more accomplished in less time.

Time Blocking

We all have the same time resource. Each one of us has 24 hours in a day, no more and no less. How you spend that time is what makes one person more productive than another. But how do you spend your 24 hours integrating all your roles? I have used the idea of time blocking. It is very simple. I just block out time in my days for certain roles and focus on those activities. When the children are at school, my time is blocked for all my professional roles. However, when the children are at home in the evening, I block out that time to spend with them.

This works sometimes, but reality often demands I play many roles at the same time. This is when time blocking interfaces with multitasking. We run a family farm. The children help with farm chores. My eight-year-old son and I have an evening routine of feeding the animals. He loves to climb in the hayloft and throw down hay. So each evening, he helps by throwing down the hay. Then while I feed the animals, he sits up in the loft talking about his day. We have developed a routine of blocking out time together and getting farm chores done.

Not all of our roles can blend as easily. I also am a writer. I have written many pages with my three year old on my lap. However, most of my writing is done at night when the children are asleep. I have blocked out time to write each evening. It is my time. Focus is the key with time blocking. But it all starts with goals, priorities, and organization.

The Harvest

Remember to enjoy the harvest. Enjoy the bounty of your work. Take the time to enjoy the moments of your life. Reward yourself. Unlike a farm, we are fortunate enough in our personal and professional lives to enjoy the bounties of our harvest daily. Each day, take time to enjoy your life, reflect on your blessings, and reward yourself.

You deserve the best.

ABOUT CYNTHIA MUSTAINE HETTINGER

Cynthia's humor, insight and down to earth advice have transformed hundreds of people's lives. Called "The Permission Giver" by her clients, Cynthia has demonstrated processes for success in personal development, sales and business ownership. She has a bias for action and believes that everyone has the internal resources to reach their life goals. Cynthia's experience includes selling financial planning, advertising, retail products, training programs and livestock. She also has planned and produced national conferences for Fortune 500 Companies. Cynthia now owns three successful small businesses. She is also the author of It's Your Life, Grab It *and the* Electra's Acres *Children's Series. Along with writing books and managing a livestock farm, Cynthia presents keynotes and workshops on sales, small business strategy, goals and personal development. Her presentations offer systematic processes, however, her stories will have you laughing. Cynthia compares the business world to her livestock through humorous and unforgettable stories. Cynthia and her husband Tony reside on their family farm in Markle, Indiana, along with their three children and over 100 farm animals.*

Contact Information
Cynthia Mustaine Hettinger
Electra's Acres
9374 North Marzane Road
Markle, IN 46770
Phone: 260-638-0050
E-Mail: electrasacres@aol.com
Website: www.electrasacres.com

THE QUICKEST WAY TO ACHIEVE YOUR FINANCIAL GOALS

By Chad Terry

Imagine being out to sea on a ship when the captain comes over the loud speaker and announces: "I have some good news and some bad news. The bad news is that we had a mishap on the bridge causing our engines to malfunction and our communications to short circuit. The good news is that we have a steady tide, and if we float long enough we are bound to find land somewhere."

I don't know about you, but I would be concerned by this news. Yet people are frequently floating along like this ship — directionless, off course, and pushed along by the tides of circumstance.

Are you lost at sea when it comes to your financial goals? What are they? How are you going to achieve your goals and how long will it take? Not sure of what your goals are? Then follow along as we plot the course for the quickest way to achieve your financial goals. The formula is as follows:

1. Dream It.
2. Plan It.
3. Dream It.

"What is the quickest way to achieve your financial goals?" I still remember being asked that question as if it happened moments ago. There I was, sitting in class on the first day of a new semester with 300 of my college classmates. The professor walked in the door, past the lectern, and slowly proceeded past the rows of students. Then he stopped next to me, looked me in the eyes and said, "What is the quickest way to achieve your financial goals?"

Taken completely off guard, I sat there in total silence, my mind desperately searching for the right answer, without success. Seeing my discomfort, the professor chuckled and asked me two more questions. "What is your greatest dream . . . and more importantly . . . how are you going to achieve it?" Smiling to himself, he turned and walked to the chalkboard. On the board he wrote in big letters DREAM IT, PLAN IT, DREAM IT.

Little did I know at the time how that formula would prove to be one of the most valuable lessons that I learned in college. It may also be one of the most important lessons you learn, as well.

Dream It.

"The way I see it, there are two kinds of dreams. One is a dream that's always going to be just that . . . a dream. A vision that you can never really hold in your hand. Then there's a dream that's more than a dream. It's like . . . a map. A map that you live by and follow for the rest of your days, knowing that someday you're going to stand on top of that mountain holding everything you thought of Right There In Your Hand!"

— Robert Cooper

Joseph Campbell said, "A dream is your creative vision for your life in the future. A goal is what specifically you intend to make happen. Dreams and goals should be just out of your present reach but not out of sight. Dreams and goals are coming attractions in your life."

Interpreting these two statements helps to define what is meant by, *Dream It*. First, dare to dream of what could be and what you want to achieve. Then, decide on which of those dreams are visions better left to the imagination and which are goals you intend to make happen. Those dreams that you commit to pursue will fill you with a sense of purpose, focus, and direction. I have found that when people are committed or passionate about something, they strive to make those goals come true. By dreaming, you are opening the door of possibilities of what can be. By committing to goals, you are taking the first step through the doorway to making them a reality. Pursuing your goals is the first step to achieving your financial goals.

Write down your financial goals. Write down each goal with as much clarity and detail as you can. Be specific. Be sure to include when you are going to make this goal become a reality. List everything you dream about, then go back and rank each one in order of priority and commit yourself to fulfilling that number one goal. Nothing will make your goals become reality faster than focusing daily on what you decide to accomplish or achieve.

Here are the steps to follow.

1. Dream
2. List your goals in detail
3. Prioritize your goals in order of importance
4. List your time horizon to accomplish your number one goal
5. List your current financial resources available to fund your goal
6. Determine how much additional money or resources are needed
7. Create a plan to achieve your stated goals

Plan It.

I cannot emphasize enough how important it is to create your plan for reaching your goals, or as I call it, your Map for Success. Without a plan you are like the ship in the opening example, directionless and pushed along by the tides of circumstance. This is an invaluable tool, but most people fail to properly plan and therefore slow their progress to reaching their goals.

According to the Retirement Confidence Survey dated April 2003, "More time (was) spent on fun than finances: Both workers and retirees say they spent more time in the past year planning for holidays and social events than planning for retirement." "Sixty-one percent of workers . . . have not calculated how much money they will need to save by the time they retire."

To further the thought, it is estimated that 87 percent of small businesses fail within the first five years. Although there are many different factors that contribute to business failure, improper or inadequate planning can certainly play a significant part. It takes a commitment to your dreams to start, but it requires a great plan to make your dreams a reality.

Map for Success

Now that you have your goals listed, how much will you need to save each month in order to achieve your goal? Most goals will require you to have sufficient financial resources and proper planning to achieve them. Your Map for Success is where you combine your goals with the actual financial needs, or a budget. Many people cringe at the thought of a budget, but you would be amazed at how effective it can be in achieving your financial goals.

Become Your Own Chief Financial Officer (CFO)

Look closely at successful companies and you will find that they keep detailed records on every aspect of their business: Sales, income, profitability, and certainly expenses. They monitor and hold accountable every department and segment of the company to help meet the overall goals of the company. Companies project their sales and the profitability of new products or campaigns carefully. The officers of the business, especially the chief financial officer (CFO), are held accountable for the performance of the company. After evaluating each alternative, they commit themselves to pursuing those products or services that offer the greatest opportunity to make the company's goals become reality.

In many ways, you are the CFO of your personal finances and should hold yourself accountable. When you are faced with decisions about whether or not to make a purchase or an investment of time or money, first decide if that action will help further your goals. As CFO, you will need to regularly monitor each portion of your map for success to ensure you are on track and make adjustments when necessary.

If you have never used a budget before, don't worry. You may find it beneficial to visit a local library or bookstore and find a book on the budgeting process. I also recommend trusted advisors, such as CPA's, accountants, and financial advisors. These professionals have specialized tools, training, and knowledge to get you started in the right direction. In addition, they may be able to provide information that will actually decrease the time needed to reach your goals.

In order to save both time and money in the long run, create an organizational system so that you can easily store, reference, and retrieve your information when necessary. The more organized you are, the quicker the process will be and the more time you can spend doing the activities you enjoy. If you are thinking that this process may take some time, you are right, but it will be time well spent.

Now that you have a plan with clearly stated goals and the map to guide you, start to follow it today. When it comes to making a financial decision, let your plan guide you to making the right decision based upon your stated goals and priorities. Continually monitor your progress. At first this may take some time to become accustomed to, but if you are diligent you will find that it will take less time and energy to maintain. Start by looking at your Map for Success daily for the first two weeks and then weekly thereafter or as needed. This seemingly simple tool is powerful beyond belief. Kim Robinson, a colleague of mine says, "Once you open yourself up to the possibilities, the cosmos will conspire to make things happen."

A Word About Debt

In some cases, you may find yourself with more expenses than income. If this is the case, start by looking for ways to decrease your expenses. I have never met a person who reached his goals and maintained them long term by spending more than he made. The quickest way to veer from reaching your goals is by acquiring large amounts of debt. By debt, I consider a reasonable mortgage and car payment acceptable. As a rule of thumb, these two expenses should not exceed 30 to 40 percent of your monthly income. In my opinion, it is the use of high interest rate credit cards and loans that are the most detrimental to your goals. Consider calling your credit card companies and requesting a lower interest rate on your existing cards to lower your expenses.

Dream It.

"Dream It, Plan It, Dream It." The first two parts of the formula are clear. Pick your goals, focus, and ensure that all your decisions and actions contribute to reaching your goals. I will confess that it took time for me to fully understand the last part of this formula. Yet, over time and with experience, I have found that you must continue to dream. Dreaming about your goals keeps you committed and on the road to achieving them. It also keeps your eyes and senses open to opportunities that can propel you even faster towards your target.

Sometimes, life throws us curve balls that alter our dreams and change our perspective. At such times, *Dream It* becomes increasingly important. I discovered how much after meeting with Jim and hearing his story. In the 1980's, Jim was a contractor in the housing industry. Business was booming and he and his family lived a comfortable lifestyle. Then, the economy started to slow, interest rates skyrocketed, and real estate sales dropped. As Jim's income dwindled, it became increasingly difficult for him to make his credit payments to the banks for construction loans. Before long, the banks repossessed all of his construction sites, materials, equipment, and even his home. He and his family were left with virtually nothing.

Fast-forward to today and you will find that Jim and his family are financially successful and happy. When I asked Jim how he recovered from such a devastating situation, he sat there for a few minutes as if lost in deep thought. As he answered with a voice full of emotion, he said that his faith and his commitment to supporting his family carried him through.

As I questioned him further, I discovered that even when faced with a devastating situation, Jim readjusted his goals, updated his plan, and never looked back. Once he reached his goals, he just kept on dreaming and has far surpassed where he had set his sights. Continue to dream and update your plans as life dictates. If Jim went from rags to riches, you can too.

Tips for Working Smarter Not Harder With your Finances

Technology

To maximize the benefits of your Map for Success, you must have the means to update and track your information. Computer software programs such as Microsoft Money or Quicken are great tools if you are comfortable working with a computer. Actually, using this software is a great time saver because you can quickly update your records. Even more convenient is the ability to download your credit card and check transactions directly from the Internet into your software, which makes it easy to categorize each transaction in your plan. That way, it may only take a few minutes a week to maintain your plan and quickly alert yourself when something needs to be addressed or an opportunity presents itself.

The use of personal digital assistants (PDAs) also helps people keep track of their expenses and due dates for bills. Paying bills on time can be a significant money saver. I once worked with a couple that consistently paid their bills late. As I helped them to create their Map for Success, I found that they paid in excess of five hundred dollars in late fees in the course of three months. Most of these expenses were the result of late fees paid to credit card companies, which averaged $30 per occurrence. It wasn't a lack of funds that caused them to be late with their payments, but a lack of organization and attention to their overall financial health.

The invention of online services being offered by banks and institutions are revolutionizing the way we manage our finances. Features and services, such as online balance transfers, allow people to transfer funds from one account to another and manage their money more efficiently. Bill paying services are also becoming a valuable tool for managing expenses and avoiding costly late fees. By using secure websites, account holders can pay their bills directly without the need for writing a check and therefore avoiding the uncertainties caused by mailing a check.

In some cases, banks will offer special discounts on mortgage or loan rates if the monthly payment is set up to be automatically paid from your account. Every cost-saving measure, no matter how small, frees up money to be used to fund your goals and dreams.

Professional Advice

Your professional advisors, such as financial planners, accountants, CPA's and some attorneys, are great resources for creating and implementing a plan for your financial success. Their expertise can help you find tax savings, unnecessary expenses, and provide education and guidance that you may desire. Finding someone that you trust is important. Many professionals will offer their services for an hourly fee without requiring clients to purchase products. Beware of advisors who immediately start telling you about the latest product. They should first find out what you are trying to accomplish, get an understanding of your values and needs, and then make appropriate suggestions for your needs. Including the use of retirement plans, planning for college needs, and much more.

What is the quickest way to achieve your financial goals? "Dream It, Plan It, Dream It." Those words spoken so many years ago by my professor hold great power and have made all the difference in my life. Dare to dream, identify your goals, and commit yourself to achieving them by creating and following your Map for Success. Invest both time and energy on yourself and you will find that your goals are closer than they appear.

The Quickest Way to Achieve Your Financial Goals (an example)

1. Dream It.
2. Plan It.
3. Dream It.
4. Do It.

Money saving tips

- Have your employer directly deposit a portion of each paycheck to your savings account and retirement accounts.
- Consider purchasing homeowners and auto insurance from the same insurer to take advantage of discounts.
- Use employer-sponsored flexible benefit programs to save money on expenses such as child care and medical bills.
- Use online bill paying services.
- Pay bills on time to avoid late fees.
- Consider annual payment if it reduces your overall expenses.
- Handle documents in a timely fashion and stay organized.
- Ask for a lower interest rate for your credit or bank cards.
- Check your credit report at least once a year to make sure information is accurate. In-accurate information can cause a lower

credit score, which may increase loan rates or eliminate eligibility for discount programs.

- Maximize your employer's match to company retirement programs.
- Consider a short-term second mortgage on your home if you finance an automobile, since the interest is tax deductible.
- Save today. According to the Bureau of Economic Analysis's report, "Personal Income and Its Disposition," personal savings for Americans averaged only 3.7% of their income in 2002.
- Start planning for your children's college education as early as possible. Apply for grants and scholarships early. Millions of dollars go unclaimed each year.
- Use specialists to help you create and monitor your plan.

ABOUT CHAD TERRY

Chad Terry is the founder and president of Financially Speaking, a company that works with organizations that invest in their people and with people who invest in their future. With a background in finance and money management, he delivers programs that are entertaining, insightful, and packed with valuable solutions for simplifying the complex world of finance. His most requested programs are Protecting Yourself from Identity Theft, Who's Getting In Your Wallet, *and* Savvy Seniors. *He is the author of* Who's Getting In Your Wallet?, How to Benefit From the Five Truths About Money *and* Protect Yourself from Identity Theft. *Chad earned his nickname of "Mr. Identity Theft" for his efforts to educate organizations and people alike about the threats of identity theft and to provide his valuable tools of protection.*

Chad's passion for helping people is clear. As a Certified Senior Advisor (CSA) he specializes in providing education and advice on key financial issues facing senior citizens. As a member of Kiwanis International, he volunteers to help benefit the children of the world.

Contact Information:
Chad Terry, CSA
Financially Speaking
15053 Rosewood Drive
Clive, IA 50325
Phone: (515) 778-0292
E-mail: chad@financiallyspeaking.biz
Website:www.financiallyspeaking.biz

CUSTOMERTHINK: *Secrets of Thinking and Acting to Differentiate your Business*

By Greg Jordan

I invited three agents from local realty companies to explain how they would market my house. My plan was to interview each one separately and list the house with the best. In my neighborhood, contractors were busily building brand new homes, creating competition for the same buyers who might consider my three-year-old home. I needed a unique and effective marketing approach.

I met with them individually — all were on time, experienced, confident and, successful real estate sales people. As they discussed their sales and marketing plans, I asked them: "So what advantage do I get by listing my home with you?"

In responding to this question, two of the agents apparently believed that the reputation of their big company was the obvious answer to my question. I could detect a slight, indignant ha-rumph! In their almost identical answers: "I will work hard to sell your house" they said; "doing everything that agents in this area normally do." What!!?? They couldn't at least pretend that they were trying to differentiate themselves? I didn't want the same old ways, I needed different. I politely sent them on their way, mentally clicking the delete button. One of them called two days later to recommend a sales price, the other left a manila envelope outside my front door with similar information, which I didn't notice for another few days.

The third interview was different. This agent seemed to be genuinely interested in my personal plans, needs, and what I was trying to accomplish. She handed me a spiral bound notebook with comparable home prices in the area, pictures and descriptions of my home already in it, and pictures and phone numbers of her entire team. She even included helpful advice, such as how to make undone laundry and other unsightly things disappear in 10 minutes for a showing. She described how she would communicate with me every week, e-mail procedures, plans she had for working with other agents, and much more.

I was impressed. She didn't even give me an opportunity to ask about the advantages for listing with her — she had already shown me. She left with my listing and my confidence in her and her team.

The lesson here is that going beyond customer expectations differentiates and builds business.

Recently I stood in a long line at a movie theater's concession stand, frustrated because I was missing the start of the movie. I expected to be able to buy tickets and get through the concession line in less than 10 minutes. This experience was taking much longer. I was trapped in a plodding concession line forced to choose between seeing the whole movie, or having popcorn and gummy bears for part of the movie . . . "Why don't they hire more people?," a fellow detainee grumbled. As I studied the situation a bit further, I realized that the employees behind the counter didn't seem to care about our plight, or the spilled popcorn mess that people had to step around. I flashed back to a previous visit to this same theater when I had stepped in the dreaded sticky spilled drink in front of my seat. It had stuck to the bottom of my shoe for at least two hours, accenting my walk with a loud and rhythmic squerrrrch! Standing in that slow line, I wondered why I had given them a second chance, and right there, resolved to find myself a new theater.

Of course, I could have gotten to the theater earlier, but when I did arrive it was clear that a bit more efficiency and caring by management and employees would have been helpful to me — the customer. Unfortunately, this story is too often replicated with services, offices, and companies. It happens despite framed slogans on the walls that declare how important customers and employees are. Empty slogans create customer cynicism and dissatisfaction. Unhappy customers take their business where they have fewer problems, often leaving the offending business unaware of the problem and with a slow leak of revenue. Conversely, people delight in finding a business that treats them like they matter, and one that works hard to keep them satisfied. These customers return and brag about the product and service to their friends — priceless advertising!

A former CEO of SAS Airlines helped his employees understand the concept of "moments of truth." Every contact that any SAS employee had with someone outside SAS was a moment of truth, whether it was the baggage claim person, a ticket agent, pilot, or a flight attendant walking the corridors of O'Hare airport. Most importantly, people made judgments about the company from these moments of truth.

In this chapter we will explore Customerthink — a systematic approach that results in positive moments of truth becoming the norm. As a mindset, Customerthink is relentlessly exceeding customer expectations. It simultaneously benefits the customer and differentiates the company, creating new levels of customer loyalty. It can be applied to any size or type of company. Customerthink is also a work process with defined elements that are implemented over time.

It's easy to see the potential for Customerthink:

The Q100 is a group of S&P 500 companies that score high in quality measures and enjoy some competitive advantages. A shorthand definition of quality includes customer focus, employee involvement and reduced defects — some of the Customerthink elements. Q100 companies' stock consistently outperforms the S&P Index. The American Society of Quality estimates that 15 to 30 percent of all costs are due to poor quality. Q100 companies bite big chunks out of these costs while improving customer satisfaction.

The University of Michigan annually measures consumer satisfaction on a broad range of products and services. Today the measure stands at 70 out of 100 — not much change in the 10 years since it has been tracked. Big companies and small alike have been unable to close this gap successfully. The opportunity for companies that can exceed customer expectations is obvious.

Companies that emphasize customer service are finding that it pays in real dollars and cents. As an example, UPS instituted a policy for all its drivers to spend 30 minutes a week talking to customers in their area, answering questions, and discovering needs. They also offered an incentive to their drivers as part of the "Sales Lead Incentive Program." Within a short period of beginning these two changes, UPS drivers had created more than 200,000 sales leads. The success rate for turning those leads into new customers was 43 percent, adding nearly $60 million in new revenue.

Companies that take their eyes off of serving their customers find themselves in high weeds with missed opportunity. When United Airlines declared bankruptcy, they were in the bottom or last in customer measures such as on time arrival and baggage delivery. Certainly, there were larger industry issues at play, but a Customerthink approach would have helped them greatly. Since that time, United has now focused on on time arrivals and now claim first in the industry on that measure. They are on the road to recovery with a customer focus.

The United States is about to make a major change in the wireless communications industry called "number portability." It will allow consumers to change wireless phone companies and keep their current phone number. Wireless providers are in a tizzy. They are offering special prices, deals, phones and anything else they can throw in so that they can prevent customer switching. What if they had pursued a Customerthink strategy all along? My bet is that they would have to worry a lot less about lost customers because they never would have given their customers a reason to switch.

There is a double benefit for small companies to use Customerthink. Fast and excellent service and lower costs allow smaller companies to compete with larger competitors. The real estate company that won my business was not the largest in town. Likewise, veterinarians usually have small practices. But many people will drive miles out of their way, often passing more convenient locations, to find a veterinarian who treats pets and pet owners alike with these principles.

Successful businesses of any size or type continuously ask themselves:

- How do I create new, and maintain existing, customers in an increasingly competitive business environment?
- How can I create long term customer loyalty in these times of higher levels of customer expectations?

What if solutions to these questions could be achieved without much technology, or additional staff or cost? Impossible? Not if real estate agents, wireless providers, airlines, package delivery services, veterinarians, and theater managers would devote themselves to implementing the five elements of the Customerthink process:

The Customerthink Model

There are uses for each of these elements separately, but when used together properly, it creates an organization that displays a LASER-esque quality — a directional, high energy, beam of light focused on exceeding customer needs.

Positive Internal Attitudes and Values

Attitudes are habits of thought that hover just below the conscious level. They are formed by repeatedly observing and associating pleasure or pain with certain actions. They differ from an opinion, in that, while our opinions may change relatively rapidly from day to day or week to week, our attitudes tend to be a little bit more fixed. Internal attitudes are related to our core values, which act as our personal judge on what is right or wrong. Together, they act without conscious thought as internal guides for decisions and behaviors. They are a direct link between the way we think and the way we behave. Therefore, in order to behave consistently and automatically to exceed customers' needs, people must internalize Customerthink attitudes and values.

Let me give you an example of attitudes in action:

As a consultant I have worked with groups of people who professed to be interested in "becoming an effective team." In one case, through a team diagnostic tool, we found that the members of the groups did not really view themselves as a team. Their basic attitude seemed to be one that valued a group identity, but supported too many individual, independent actions that often caused conflict later. Before there could be any progress, the group needed a different view of themselves as a team — a different attitude towards their teamness.

So how does one develop the right attitudes?

Business owners and leaders must begin by examining their own personal habits of thought and values, and those of the organization. They must decide if they are consistently aligned with generating customer loyalty and if not, put new ones in place by defining and communicating them and expressing them through their own actions, every single day. The hard work is in communicating and demonstrating the changes over the long haul and consistently rewarding behaviors that align with them. Leaders become guardians of values and attitudes, and coaches to help others understand and align.

Recognition of employees' effort and incentive programs are two particularly effective tools to help new attitudes take root. The opposite is also true. Behaviors that do not reflect Customerthink principles must be eliminated either through coaching of the employee or dismissal. An employee sitting behind a customer service desk, absorbed in paperwork, ignoring a waiting customer cannot be tolerated because it's at odds with the attitudes and values of Customerthink.

Consistently paying attention to the right internal attitudes and values provides a guide and a compass, producing the necessary behaviors.

Goal Setting and Planning

If attitudes and values act as the compass leading to greater customer loyalty, then goals and actions are the maps providing landmarks, distances, and topography. Clear, measurable Customerthink goals must be in place, understood, and acted upon by everyone. The best attitudes will be short lived if people don't have an effective way to implement them. All goals must relate back to the vision, mission and core values of the organization. If they do not exist, they must be created. If they do exist, they must be revised to reflect the new direction.

People often think about goals as something larger than life — the put-the-man-on-the-moon-in-ten-years type. Actually it's simpler. Successful people and organizations have specific, measurable, and time -bound goals with action plans that become the centerpiece of the organization's activities. Here is an outline for establishing Customerthink goals and action plans that can be used for setting and achieving personal and organizational goals. It is important to involve key thought leaders in this process.

1. On five separate sheets of paper, label each according to the following titles: Customer Satisfaction, Business Process Improvement, New Customer Products/ Benefits, Product Cost Reduction, Internal Attitudes and Values.
2. Write down goals that are needed to exceed customer expectations in each area. Make sure they follow the SMART guide-

lines: specific, measurable, achievable, realistic and time-bound.

3. Select the three most important goals from each list.
4. Select the three to four most important goals from step 3.
5. Write each goal on a separate page.
6. Plan the goal — On each page, write the benefits of achieving the goal, the consequences of not achieving the goal, the potential barriers that would be in the way, and what actions need to be taken, by whom and by when.
7. Communicate these goals and plans to everyone inside the organization and to your customers (condense it for customers).
8. Periodically review progress with the action plan owners and make adjustments where necessary.
9. Recognize and reward progress.

Continuous Business Process Improvement (CBPI)

Do not be intimidated by this long term and acronym. CPBI is simply a common sense efficiency system that streamlines the way work is done. It is the business equivalent of improving PC speed dramatically by clearing the hard drive of temporary files. Customers always benefit when your operations are continuously improved.

CPBI is an adaptation of a Toyota-originated process that created a competitive advantage in cost and other areas, such as reduced times from order to delivery and shorter new car development times. It is a major reason why the Big Three from Detroit have now become the Big Five with recent gains by Toyota and Honda. The good news is that the same concepts can be applied to any size or type of business. The most important element is an eternal commitment to learn and continuously improve.

CBPI blends Total Quality, and a form of Lean thinking, Cycle Time Reduction. What these fancy titles do together is to remove any activity or step that is more than the minimum required to perform a task. Constant elimination of non-value-added activities creates faster service, higher quality and lower costs that benefit both the customer and the company.

The central CBPI process applied in Customerthink is the continuous removal of seven wastes, described below. As you read through them, visualize how it might be applied to your business whether it's a small, one-person office or a large corporation. Then take a "Waste Walk" around your office and identify opportunities for improvement. A team approach is even more effective at solving the kinds of problems you will undoubtedly find.

1. Overproduction — Making or doing more than is required

Mentally picture the episode of Lucy and Ethel trying unsuccessfully to wrap candy from a production line as it increased in speed and you have the essence of overproduction. It creates waste and inventory. The production products of an office environment are decisions, information, planning, policies and procedures. When decisions are not made on time, or too much information is sent out to too many people, it creates a logjam and slows office processes down, to the sorrow of waiting customers. Is there excess effort and/or time spent producing stuff?

A Fortune 500 company that I worked for initiated a leadership development program in which each person invited multiple people to fill out several long feedback forms for one another. Hundreds of people became involved in this internal process that tied up the management team, and at times distracted them from the main business of serving customers. I am all for people development, but we should have found a less involved process that kept the right balance for staff and customers.

2. Inventory — An accumulation in excess of what's needed

Inventory is costly. Examples of office environment inventory are paperwork, meetings, supplies, e-mails, and decisions. Excess amounts of these elements interfere with the smooth flow of work. How much time is spent looking for stuff because of piles of paperwork on desks waiting to be processed? I had a client who lost my invoice for some consulting work — they looked for it for two days — and then called me back and asked me to resend the invoice. Then I had to stop what I was doing to regenerate the invoice. What can be done to reduce the accumulated paperwork, decisions or other materials? Does every meeting add value?

3. Waiting — Delays in the work process

Customers expect increasingly quick service. Industries as varied as banking, internet service providers, and fast food restaurants understand this and work hard to meet this need. For example, at McDonalds they know that customers get irritated if they wait more than 2 to 3 minutes for their food. Delays cost time and money. Is customer wait time an important measure? Where are you making your customer wait? What are the root causes of these delays? What can you start, stop, or eliminate to reduce or eliminate wait times?

4. Transportation — Excess movement of material or information

Anytime there is a need to move product, paperwork, or information from one place to another, it's an opportunity for loss, damage, and delay. In a manufacturing environment this is often easy to see. In an office, it's harder to see. Mapping out the way information, materials or decisions get made yields insights that can make the operation faster and more efficient. An associate of mine owned a medical transcription business. The five transcriptionists had to drive to the doctor's office, pick up voice tapes, drive back to their homes, transcribe and type, and then drive the completed documents back to the doctor's office. They now use digital recordings transmitted from the doctor's office over the internet, type it, and send it back via e-mail — saving transportation costs and reducing wait times — a real customer benefit and lower costs for the business. Where do you have stuff moving around unnecessarily? And the cardinal sin of them all — moving stuff more than once? How can some of this waste be eliminated?

5. Motion — Movement of people, machines or information that does not add value

Ski jumpers and world class sprinters know that any wasted motion — any body part that is out of place or not used efficiently — will sacrifice performance. At the movies, when the concession stand operators have to walk back and forth to fill a customer's order, often crossing one another's path, it wastes time, risks spilled drinks and popcorn, and makes some customers miss the previews. Why not redesign the counter for employees to make it possible for most, if not all products to be within arm's reach without walking? Do people have all the tools they need without walking across the room or to the warehouse? Should the office, plant or store layout be redesigned to reduce steps, or reaching?

6. Processing — Excess effort that adds no value

Look closely at the number of steps in producing your products. Is there really a need for so many forms to fill out? I was working with an electrical products company on cycle time reduction, taking them through removal of the seven wastes from their showroom — sales — warehouse work process. As we mapped their process, step by step to look at who was doing what, where were there delays, a salesman said: "I spend 50 percent of my time in the office doing paperwork" — a stunning revelation from the person who brought in revenue and serviced customers. His teammates didn't even realize the magnitude of the problem. Not only was he unable to spend quality time with his customers, they were losing sales. This wasn't a Customerthink operation. When they changed the work process to eliminate some of the paperwork and assign what was left to other staff, the freed-up salesman picked up three new major accounts within a month. Where is your company overprocessing and losing opportunity? Can the operation be simplified? Is there a valid reason for every step that people take in the process?

7. Defects — Rework or problems due to not meeting customer needs

Defects can be the easiest of the seven wastes for customers to see. Only if it is measured can you make sustained progress in reducing defects. Anything that does not meet the needs of a customer is a defect. This includes internal customers since many times within a company, one department may be the customer of another. In an office environment, not achieving goals, objectives, or action plans is a defect. So are not achieving meeting objectives, missed dates, budget overruns, actions inconsistent with core values, and customer complaints. The root causes of defects must be systematically discovered and eliminated. It is best if this effort involves important suppliers and partners. Who are your internal and external customers? How do you know when you are meeting their needs? What can be done today to eliminate a single cause of customer dissatisfaction?

Innovative Products and Services

As part of a talk that I gave to a home remodeling association, my research turned up in the *Wall Street Journal*, a new term called "Serial Renovation." Homeowners are replacing entire rooms in their homes before they wear out. Kitchens, bathrooms, master suites, and family rooms are being overhauled 33 percent faster than 10 years ago. Remodeling business owners who understand these trends can begin to serve their customers better by creating new services and products that meet homeowner needs.

No matter the size or type of business, it needs to constantly upgrade products and services to stay competitive. Like faster service, customers expect a certain level of continuous product or service upgrades. If your business does not provide them, it can quickly lose the competitive edge. Take a stroll down an aisle in a hotbed of innovation — the grocery store. Companies have created green ketchup, new pizza cutters, frozen gourmet meals, flavored colas, double stuffed Oreos, new cereals, etc. Even the store format has changed so that shoppers can get just about anything they need, from a home cooked meal to a money order. I would argue that not all of these are good things, but the point is that the grocery industry has the innovation religion.

Make sure that there is a process in place for your company to discover trends, new technologies, and ideas that you can copy to serve your customers better.

Customers have an entirely different view of your company if they know that you are constantly striving to upgrade your products, services, and skills. They expect novel approaches and products, and have a sense that they will be of value to them.

Leadership

Leadership balances and holds the elements of Customerthink together. Today's leadership definition places a priority on the ability to achieve goals and objectives through all available resources.

Effective leadership has two roles — managing and leading. The managing role constantly tests results, direction, and pace of goals and action plans. Reading the map, checking current direction, and making mid-course corrections are important functions. Managing keeps the effort moving forward efficiently.

The leading role defines goals, attitudes, values, and priorities for the business. They embody the attitudes and values, encourage and energize people, and create accountability. Most importantly, leaders insure that the culture is changing in a way that supports Customerthink. They bring a sense that this is a long-term commitment, not the program of the month. Constant communication of progress, successes, learnings and gaps, along with handing out rewards for contributors, are all elements of the leadership role. Without effective leadership, even if it is self-leadership, none of this will happen.

I would encourage you to take a new look at your business in light of the Customerthink Model. It's certainly not an easy task to put all of this in place in a quality way, but ask yourself, "What will happen to our business if competition adopts it before we do?" and, "How much better could we serve our customers by implementing these 5 elements?"

If that theater that I referred to at the beginning of this chapter would adopt both the tools and spirit of Customerthink . . .

- Positive Internal Attitudes
- Goal Setting and Planning
- Continuous Business Process Improvement
- Innovative Products and Services
- Effective Management and Leadership

. . . they would see that criss-crossing walking patterns behind the concession counter are non-value-added motions that lead to defects (missed customer expectations). They would rearrange their workspace to eliminate waste and reduce customer wait time. They would regard a sticky floor as a defect that must be removed right away, and would have clear goals of customer satisfaction. They would project an attitude that they are there to help provide an entertainment experience for their customer. Ideas for how to reduce costs while maintaining a good entertainment experience would flow from theater goers, employees, and management.

Since this is a lot to ask from a 16-year-old, management would have to see that all of this would happen and would constantly be looking for new ways to create a positive entertainment experience for me — that's right, me — that paying customer, constantly looking for the ultimate customer experience.

ABOUT GREG JORDAN

Greg Jordan has been in Fortune 500 corporate leadership positions for over 20 years. He gained broad industry experience in leading organization transformations and launching new products in the Energy Utilities, Pulp and Paper, Orange Juice Processing, Disposable Diapers, Health Care, and Appliances industries.

He started Peak Performance Solutions in the year 2000, as a management consulting firm that helps people and organizations accomplish significantly improved results.

Contact Information:
Greg Jordan
Peak Performance Solutions Inc.
Phone: (515) 554 4305
E-mail: greg@peak-ps.com
Website: www.peak-ps.com

Put it in Perspective: A Guide to Managing Those Everyday Stressors

by Lynn Hauser

What is the biggest source of your stress? Think about it and write it here ______________________________.

What did you write? The job? The spouse? The kids? Too much to do and not enough time? Not enough money? There's only one thing that should be written in the box — myself. That's correct. We are the biggest source of our own stress. All of those other things are stressors.

Stressors are the people and things in our world to which we respond with feelings of stress. Put another way, stress is not what happens to us; stress is how we react to what happens to us. This is the key concept to managing our stress more effectively. As long as we continue to blame our stress on something or someone else, we may be powerless to do anything about it because we may not control the something or someone else. When we realize that our stress comes from how we react to the stressor and not the stressor itself, we can control our stress because we can control our reaction. It's not always easy, but we can do it if we choose. When we begin to take control over our reaction to what happens to us, we stop becoming victims of our stressors.

The first step in getting a handle on our stress is to understand that we are the source of our stress. The second step is to identify all the important stressors we have in our lives. When you identify your stressors, it's important to be as specific as possible. What, exactly, is it that you're responding to with feelings of stress? If, for example, you identify your job as a stressor, where do you start to fix it? It's just too big to get a handle on. But if you break that job up into smaller pieces, you can now determine the real issue: you're expected to work 70 hours a week; the work is boring and unchallenging; your personal values don't fit into the corporate culture; you don't like your boss.

The same is true if your stressor is a person. The stressor really isn't the person; it's something the person is doing . . . it's a behavior. Once you break the stressor down into the smallest possible pieces, it's less overwhelming and a little easier to manage. You can learn to change your reactions to deal with one smaller issue at a time.

Take the time now to identify your top 5 stressors. These are the ones that bother you the most. You may have more than 5, but just start there for now. Remember, be very specific.

My Top 5 Stressors

1.____

2.____

3.____

4.____

5.____

Now that you've identified your top five stressors, take a moment to think about how you usually react to that stressor. In order to manage your stress more effectively, you must become aware of your normal response to the stressor. What thoughts and feelings do you have when the stressor occurs? Are you angry, defensive, or happy? What behaviors do you normally exhibit? Do you yell, scream, cry, use positive self-talk, meditate, or do you choose to do nothing?

Write your typical reaction in terms of feelings and behaviors in the space provided below, and then decide if the reaction is positive or negative. Is the amount of energy used appropriate for the situation? Does the feeling meet your needs over time?

Stressor	Typical Feelings	Typical Behaviors	+/-

You've probably noticed that if your feelings are negative, so are your behaviors. Brian Tracy in *The Psychology of Achievement* puts it this way, "We become what we think about most." Your thoughts turn into feelings, which lead to behaviors. Those behaviors reinforce the thoughts and feelings, leading to more behaviors. You are a self-fulfilling prophecy. If your thoughts and feelings are positive, so are the behaviors. The opposite is also true. Negative thoughts and feelings lead to negative behaviors.

If you identified your reaction to a particular stressor as positive, you are dealing with that stressor in a healthy way. If your reaction is negative, it's important to think about how you can change that reaction so it is more positive. Our reaction to stressors is often a negative emotional one. Our challenge is to stop reacting emotionally so that we can respond more logically to the situation. A logical response is one that gives the stressor the appropriate amount of time and energy based on two criteria: importance and control.

Importance — In the scheme of life, how important is the stressor? Be careful not to get too caught up in "the principle." Have you ever gotten very angry over something and, when you asked yourself why, all you could come up with is "it's a matter of principle?" While principle and living by our values are important, we sometimes use them as excuses to get angry over things that are not really important at all.

One way to determine if the stressor is really important is to use a problem-solving technique called "5 Whys." After you identify the stressor, ask yourself 5 questions as to why it is important.

For example:

Stressor — My husband doesn't fold the towels the way I want him to when he takes them out of the dryer. (I didn't make that one up; I hear it all the time.)

Why is that important? I like the towels folded a certain way.

Why? Because they fit better in the linen closet.

Do they fit in the closet his way? Yes.

So what's the problem? It's not my way.

In this example, we arrived at the real problem after only 4 questions; your husband doesn't fold the towels your way. His way works, but you want it done your way. Get over yourself! It doesn't have to be your way to be right. Instead of fussing at him because he's doing it "wrong," why not recognize the effort to help and simply say thank you. In the scheme of life, how he folds the towels is meaningless and certainly not worth the time and energy expended getting angry.

Control — Control is one of our basic life needs. Losing control over the important things in our lives is often seen as a major stressor. Do you have the power to change the stressor yourself? If not, then that stressor is out of your control.

Once you've analyzed the stressor in terms of its importance and whether or not it's within your control, you can now take the appropriate action. The following matrix will help you put that stressor into perspective and choose a more positive reaction.

Time Management Matrix

	Controllable	Not Controllable
Important		
Not Important		

Important & Controllable — I met a woman in a stress management workshop who said one of her biggest stressors was being significantly late for work on a regular basis. Is that important? You'd think so. Is it controllable? You'd think so. In fact, when the other participants asked her why she was late she gave all the usual reasons: hit the snooze alarm too many times, kids got up late, didn't have anything clean to wear to work, not enough gas in the car, had to make the kids' lunches. So, what do you do when your stressor is important and controllable? Take action. The stressor is important and within your control, so do something about it. While that may sound like a no-brainer, we don't always do it. Instead, we sit around wringing our hands, whining, crying, and wishing things were different.

Important/Not Controllable — Your manager calls an emergency department meeting and announces that your company has just merged with another, resulting in redundant functions. Some of those functions are in your department, and management is estimating that one-third of your department will be laid off in 90 days. You have a 1 in 3 chance of being out of a job in 3 months. While this stressor is important, it is one that you don't control. Someone else is going to make the decision as to who is laid off.

If your stressor fits into this category, respond with two strategies. First, use positive coping skills to help you deal with what you don't control. Positive coping skills include things like:

- Yoga
- Exercise
- Positive self-talk
- Laughter
- Massage
- Self-hypnosis
- Play with your kids
- Play with your pet
- Meditate
- Aromatherapy
- Progressive muscle relaxation

Positive coping skills help us relax and maintain a positive attitude. Research has shown that stroking a pet reduces blood pressure and eases feelings of stress. Exercise and laughter release endorphins, the body's natural feel-good hormone.

The second strategy is to find a way to regain control over the situation. Since being in control of your life and destiny is one of life's basic needs, that's really the big problem. You've lost control over whether or not you get to keep your job. If you think about it, there are many things you can do to regain some control in this situation. You can:

- Update your resume
- Start looking for a job
- Re-evaluate your professional goals
- Inventory your skills

- Go back to school
- Network
- Examine your finances; how long could you afford to be out of work?
- Cut expenses
- Ask questions; which positions are most likely to be cut?

You could also simply stop worrying about it and make yourself indispensable to the company. Volunteer for extra projects or to serve on a task force. You may be able to influence the decision in your favor. But, even if you still get laid-off, you'll have a stronger resume and will probably get a glowing recommendation from your manager. Your positive attitude during this difficult time will tell potential employers a great deal about your character and your ability to work effectively under stress.

Once you've identified how you can regain control, you've actually moved back into the first box of the matrix, important and controllable. You've found ways you can take action.

In this example, there are a number of ways to regain control, but it's not always that easy. A woman in a workshop shared this example. Several years earlier she experienced serious health problems for which she had undergone radiation and chemotherapy. She told us that she felt like her life was totally out of her control. When faced with a second round of chemotherapy she knew that she was going to lose her hair again. She decided that she wasn't going to let that happen to her, so she shaved her head. By shaving her head, she found a way to regain control. It made all the difference in the world, making what she didn't control easier to handle.

The reality is that there may be no way to regain control in some of these important but not controllable situations. Then your only option is the first strategy of positive coping skills. Whining and crying about the situation accomplishes nothing.

Not Important/Controllable — In spite of the fact that I facilitate workshops on stress management on a regular basis, I don't always get it right myself. This is hard stuff! Here's a story to illustrate this box of the matrix.

Several years ago I was facilitating a workshop on Stress Management Strategies for Women for a public seminar client. I arrived at the hotel the night before, and upon checking in, I received a copy of the most current roster for the workshop that the client had faxed to the hotel. The next morning I arrived in the meeting room at about 7:00 a.m. to prepare for a 9:00 a.m. start time. My assistant, Theresa, was setting up for registration in the back of the large ballroom while I was getting my things set up in front. When Theresa asked me for the roster, I couldn't find it. I looked in all the usual places, my briefcase, folders, etc., but alas, no roster. My immediate reaction was negative self-talk; "Are you stupid or what? You had that in your hands yesterday, now what did you do with it? You'd lose your head if it wasn't attached." I told Theresa that I couldn't find it but that I would go back up to my room to look for it. She said not to bother; she would call the client and request another copy. But no, that wasn't good enough for me. I had to find the one I had in my hand last night because I hate it when I do stupid things like that. I went back to my room; tore the place apart but . . . no roster. I never found it. Someday when we find all the socks that disappear from the dryer, we'll also find that roster. By the time I got back downstairs, I was in a rage. My head was spinning on my shoulders and smoke was pouring from my ears.

Now let's put this into perspective. In about 90 minutes there were going to be over 100 women in the room to learn how to manage their stress more effectively. I was supposed to be the expert, but what was I getting my knickers in a knot about? A roster that, by the time I got back to the ballroom, Theresa had already replaced. I had forgotten one very important thing — this stressor was not important. My reaction was emotional and way out of proportion to the situation. Theresa helped me remember this with just four words: "Lynn, let it go." It was a gentle reminder to put the situation into perspective.

Since the stressor is controllable, you can take action. Theresa did this with a simple phone call. Remember, though, that while it is controllable, it's not important. Ask yourself, is it a good use of my time to take action? If so, do it and let it go. If not, just let it go.

Not Important/Not Controllable — Then we have my all-time favorite part of the matrix. Here's another story about myself, but one I'm sure many of you will relate to. I'm in the grocery story and since I'm buying only a gallon of milk and loaf of bread I go immediately to the checkout line that says: Express Lane, 12 Items or Less.

So, I'm in line with my 2 items when I notice the woman in front of me has 16 items. How do I know that? You've got it — I counted them, and not very subtly either. I point to the items as I count just loudly enough so she'll hear me. I don't want her to think she's sliding anything past me. Then I start to mumble under my breath. "What's the matter; doesn't she know how to count or can't she read?" Even I am not bold enough to actually say anything to her, but I'm not going to let this go. Why? It's a matter of principle! She's not following the rules. So after she's paid for and walked out of the store with her 16 items, I complain to the cashier. Here's how that conversation goes:

Me: That women had 16 items her basket. This is the express line. The sign says 12 items or less.

Cashier: Well we don't control what they put on the counter. If they put it up here we have to check it out.

Me: Well then take the sign down!

Believe it or not, I've actually said that. You may laugh, but you've probably done something like that yourself. It may not have been in the grocery store, but you've done it somewhere. For you it might be swearing at the driver who doesn't do the thank-you wave when you let him merge onto the road in front of you. Or, the expressive body language you use when someone dares to drive the speed limit on the highway — in the fast lane. This box of the matrix contains our pet peeves, the little day-to-day irritants that drive us crazy. If we really think about these situations, they are neither important nor controllable. How much longer did I wait in line because that woman had 4 more items than allowed in the express line? A minute, maybe two? What's that in the scheme of life?

In an audio program called *Release It and Let It Go*, Dr. Kimberly Ventus-Darks suggests this strategy to help get us past these little irritants. Think about the importance of this person in the scheme of your life. Plot them on a scale from 1-10, with ten being the most important person in your life and one being not important at all. Then, give them the amount of energy appropriate for their place on the scale. Where does the woman in the grocery store fit? She's a negative two! I don't know her, I'll never see her again, and I couldn't pick her out of a lineup five minutes later. But, how much energy did I use in response to her behavior? How much power did I give her over me? I let her ruin those 10 minutes of my life. That's a lot of power to give a total stranger. Let's go back to the example of how your spouse folds the towels. While the person is important in your life, the situation is not. The stressors that fit in this box of the matrix are the ones not worth your time and energy to do anything about. Use your positive coping skills and stop sweating the small stuff.

Putting it all together

Where do your stressors fit in the matrix? If you're honest with yourself, most of them fall into the final three categories. They aren't important and/or they're not controllable. The only part of the matrix that's worth your time is the important/controllable box. It's the only one that matters. It's the only one with stressors that are not only within your control to change, but also important enough to worry about. You only have a finite amount of time and energy to deal with the stressors in your life; use it wisely by focusing only on the important and controllable issues.

Take another look at your top 5 stressors. Write them down in the chart below and identify the part of the matrix they fit in. Be honest and ask yourself the 5 whys to determine if they really are important or simply one of your pet peeves. Once you know where the stressor fits in the matrix, you can choose the appropriate response.

Stressor	**Matrix**	**Positive Response**

Remember, stress is not what happens to you, it's how you react to what happens to you. You may never control the stressor, but you can always control your reaction to it. Stop letting emotions rule your reactions. Stop giving people who are relatively unimportant in your life so much power over you. Stop living your life as if every little thing that happens is the most important thing in the world.

Here's another way to put it . . . stress is an attitude. No one controls your attitude but you. Your kids don't make you crazy; you choose to get crazy over something they've done. The more positive your everyday attitude, the more effective you'll be at keeping that positive attitude in times of stress. Make a conscious effort to limit your exposure to negative information — stop reading the newspaper and watching the TV news, get rid of the toxic people in your life, turn negative self-talk into positive. When you maintain a positive attitude, the little things don't seem to matter anymore and, just maybe, your positive attitude will be contagious. You'll be able to influence others more than they influence you. But if not, even if everyone else around you is negative, you can still maintain your own positive attitude. When you learn to do that, you'll be better able to put it all into perspective, and, what a wonderful life you'll have!

ABOUT LYNN HAUSER

A retired United States Navy Nurse Corps Officer, Lynn's passion is increasing organizational effectiveness through a wide range of performance improvement solutions, all customized to meet the specific needs of the client. Her consulting, training design and facilitation have assisted thousands in achieving higher levels of success.

During her 20 years on active duty, Lynn used the lessons learned as a manager to develop other navy leaders while serving as head of the department responsible for the leadership and management training of Navy physicians, nurses, dentists, administrators and allied health professionals. Since retiring, she has continued in her quest to help organizations succeed through increasing the effectiveness of their biggest asset . . . their employees.

Lynn has her M.S. in Nursing and is a member of the International Society for Performance Improvement, The American Society for Training and Development, the American Business Women's Association, the National Association for Female Executives and the National Speakers Association.

Contact Information:
Lynn Hauser
Performance Partners, Inc.
P.O. Box 757
Frankfort, IL 60423-0757
Phone: (815) 464-5472
E-mail: lynn@performancepartnersinc.net
Website: www.lynnspeaks.com

Make This Your Smartest Year Yet!

by Doug Smart, CSP

I have a friend named Mike. He lives in Metairie, Louisiana. As a storeowner he got to know many of his customers well. One man always asked Mike for a discount. Being a good businessman, he smiled, but it really bugged him. One day Mike asked the customer, "Why do you keep asking me for a discount? It's not like you need the money. You've got eight rental houses!"

The man smiled a sheepish grin and replied, "You can't blame me for asking. And besides, wherever I shop, I always ask for a discount."

"Does it work?" inquired Mike.

"Sometimes," he replied. "About ten percent of the time I get a discount."

Mike was amazed.

Does that mean you or I can walk into a store like Sears, Macy's or Dillard's, ask for a discount, and expect to get it? Sometimes! The clerk might look at you like you just fell off Jupiter, but don't be surprised to hear, "Well, okay. I'm empowered. At least that's what they tell me. I can make decisions. Come with me. We'll ring it up." And presto! It works! You know the old wisdom, "You don't ask, you don't get." Let me ask you something. In order for you to enjoy wholehearted success, isn't asking vital to getting? For example, if you are leading a sweeping change in your company, such as implementing important new procedures, don't you have to ask your co-workers to stay focused and flexible? If you are introducing new products, don't you have to ask your customers to trust you and try them? If you want to see improvement in yourself, don't you have to ask yourself to be dedicated and determined?

Here's a quick true/false quiz:

In order to work smarter, not harder . . .

- ☐ T ☐ F You have to ask yourself to be open to new information.
- ☐ T ☐ F You have to ask other people to believe in you.
- ☐ T ☐ F You have to ask yourself to believe in yourself.
- ☐ T ☐ F You want to cultivate a deep appreciation for what you already have.
- ☐ T ☐ F You have to ask yourself to try new ideas.
- ☐ T ☐ F You need to find ways to keep your energy fired up.

The answers to all are true. Asking yourself to be strong in these personal areas boosts your personal energy. To put a name on it, let's call what keeps your energy levels high your rocket fuel, or RF.

In 1963, when President John F. Kennedy asked the American people to accept his vision of a man on the moon by the end of the decade, he was really asking for the energy that comes from commitment to hard-held goals. He did not ask if it were possible (It's a good thing he didn't because the answer would have been no. At the time, the scientific community did not possess even fifteen percent of the information needed to accomplish the goal). He simply asked us to believe that his vision was possible. From the energy of that belief came the RF to do the impossible.

You and I regulate our RF every day through the constant stream of conversations in our heads. On a typical day we talk to ourselves approximately 10,000 times. However, for many of us, it is estimated as much as eighty percent of those personal 10,000 conversations have a negative tone, such as: "I can't. With my luck it'll probably rain. Nothing like that works for me." As adults, sometimes we are P.O.W. (Prisoners of Our Wishes). We get so bogged down in the impossibility of our challenges we drain off much of our RF, and what is left is diluted and polluted. Our rocket does not rise to the clouds, much less to the stars. What can we do?

I am a motivator, keynoter, consultant, author, and entrepreneur. After presenting over 1,000 presentations for organizations as diverse as Wal-Mart, Special Olympics, and the Kennedy Space Center at Cape Canaveral (hey, I have worked with real rocket scientists!), I have observed first hand that the people who seem to be secure, positive, and happy are the ones who maintain high levels of energy, confidence, and resiliency. They seem to manufacture their own RF. You can, too, with a formula for staying strong, confident, and resilient no matter what life throws in your direction.

10-20-30-40-50 Resiliency System

It's a smart idea to read for 10 minutes every morning. Ever wake up to chatter or music on the radio? Ever have the first song of the day stick in your head and you can't get it out? You're OK if it's a happy, upbeat song. But what if it's one of those depressing, spirit-draining, heart stoppers? Just as newly hatched ducks experience, early images imprinted onto an awakening brain tend to stick. Instead of gambling that good-for-you stuff will happen to stimulate your mind, take charge. For ten minutes every morning, it's a smart idea to read. Fill your head with things beneficial to you. Grab something to read that is inspirational, motivational, or "how to." For me, I love to read biographies — how did other people fight the lions, tigers, and bears of their lives? I'll grab a computer magazine. I'm not particularly computer literate, so I'll read an article to learn something new and maybe risk trying it out during the day. Or I'll grab a seed catalog. I love to garden, and it is spring in my house any morning I choose. I think that seed catalogs are the most optimistic literature on the planet — packed with optimism and the empowering message, "You can grow this too!"

You have heard the old saying, "We become what we think about," so I urge you to take control and start your day thinking of things that are beneficial to you. It is smart to put wholesome brain groceries in your head for a fresh start. Begin your day in a strong, positive way. Ignore the TV, radio, and newspaper until later — all you'll miss is a diet that might be setting you up for feeling down. And avoid getting dependent on outside media to jumpstart your feelings anyhow. Instead, take charge and read for ten minutes every morning. It's a smart start to a terrific day every day.

Spend 20 minutes a day around positive, motivated, optimistic people. They can be an instant energy source for you. And if you can't find any, go rent some! Check out motivational tapes from your training library. Motivational tapes are popular listening for success-minded people as they drive to work.

Denis Waitley, author of *The Psychology of Winning*, says, "We become the people around us." You and I want to embrace the company of people who are good for us. We want to be around people who have the energy and enthusiasm for life of a nine-year-old. Christine, our nine-year-old neighbor, crossed the street and asked, "Can I catch bugs in your garden?"

"Sure, Christine," I replied, "but why don't you catch the bugs in your garden?"

"Because my Daddy sprays," she informed me, "and he says you don't. Last night he told Mom again that the big ones must still be coming from your side."

I still chuckle when I think about it. Isn't the openness of a child refreshing? Doesn't it feel good to be around adults who still have that frankness, optimism, and energy? Don't we need to be around people who speak their minds and don't play politics or wear masks? Go find them because life does not necessarily bring them to you. Haven't you noticed that if you do not go find the good ones, the bad ones fill the void?

Other people add to or deplete your RF. You know how you feel around people who gripe and moan about how life is unfair, work stinks, and that nobody really understands them. Depressed and de-energized come to mind because they contaminate the RF. On the other hand, when you are around upbeat people who volunteer for new assignments, put in extra hours to do something well, or enthusiastically help others reach their goals, you feel renewed and re-energized. Your RF is pure and increasing in volume. Spend twenty minutes a day around optimistic people and feel their energy and charisma arc into you. Enjoy them, let them flourish in you, and arc your spare RF over to someone else.

Say 30 positive things about yourself to yourself every day. On a typical day we say 10,000 things to ourselves. Make at least thirty of them positive self-statements to build a supply of self-generating RF.

Saying positive affirmations about yourself is powerful. Three thousand years ago King Solomon noted that as a man thinks, he becomes. How often do you affirm the best in yourself? I recommend to all business people to say thirty positive things about yourselves to yourselves everyday. You want to say things that reflect your deep inner truth. Most will start with "I am." On my list I have: "I am a child of God. I am a good father. I am a doer. I am optimistic and enthusiastic. I am lucky. I am a risk-taker so that I gain security. I am an internationally known motivational speaker."

All that sounds very straightforward, but I'll tell you, it took me three months to make the list. When I first wrote down those things, I did not totally believe them.

The acid test is this: Read your list every morning while standing in front of a mirror. The hard part will be not flinching. You see, there are six billion people on Earth and you have the ability to lie to every one except one. Who's that? Yourself! If you flinch or avert your eyes, then you do not yet believe what you are telling yourself.

I want you to write out a list of thirty positive things about yourself that express the real you — both the way you are now and what you believe you are capable of becoming — and then every morning stand in front of a mirror and say those things to yourself. It's an emotionally healthy and powerful way to affirm your personal truth that your business life may have buried deep under the layers. Bring it back up. Live it!

Say "Thank you" 40 times a day. Zig Ziglar calls this "the attitude of gratitude" that affirms life is good right now. You and I have low-energy people on our teams who don't appreciate how good they have it. I suspect they see life as a stream of aggravations, challenges, and annoyances that have to be endured.

A few years ago I was standing on the curb outside the Fayetteville, Arkansas, airport waiting for a hotel shuttle to pick me up. A bright red car screeched to a halt just a few yards past me. The driver, obviously in a hurry, jumped out the second it stopped. Without looking, he reached behind himself to shut the car door. Like an errant baseball batter, he swung hard, but he totally missed the car door. He froze. His face distorted into a look of total aggravation. He stepped back, grabbed the car door at the top corner and slammed it shut — as if he were teaching that car a lesson. Then with a sour look, he stomped past me into the airport. I was just standing there on the curb with luggage at my feet waiting for a hotel shuttle, but, instantly, I felt a sensation come over me. I knew it was coming and I tried to resist, but I could not. I felt sorry for whomever it was he came to meet! There was someone in the airport excited to be coming home or arriving for business, and he was what awaited that person. I then thought, even if he were running late, he could have been grateful he was able to leave his car right at the entrance to the airport terminal.

Compare that incident to this. My plane landed in Dallas, Texas, at noon on a very hot day. When I went to get my rental car, instead of standing in long lines at the counter, I went right to the car lot. As a frequent customer, I have a card that allows me to skip the lines, proceed to a special area, and choose any car there. The paperwork is on the front seat and the keys are in the ignition. A guard checks me on the way out. It is a great system.

On that particular day, before I chose a shiny new car, I looked up at the exit and I could not help but notice there was no guardhouse. I did not see anyone to check my paperwork. "They sure are trusting in Dallas," I thought. I selected a beautiful new car, still wet from being freshly washed despite the intense heat. I backed it out, put it into drive, and as I approached the exit, I noticed a car parked on the side. Someone in a uniform was in it. The motor was running and the air conditioning was on. The guard apparently had helped herself to a new automobile, and she was using it as her office to keep cool. That had to make for a challenging day!

As I approached, a woman with a beautiful, energetic smile leapt out of the car. I pressed the brake, pressed the button to roll down my window and, without thinking, the first words that tumbled out of my mouth were, "It sure is hot out here. It must be rough working in that car all day." She looked down at me, smiled broadly and said, "It's not so bad."

A moment later, as she was checking my paperwork, she added, "I'm working sixteen hours today."

"Sixteen hours! How come?," I asked.

"Since they don't have a guardhouse," she explained, "they can't keep anybody. I don't mind. They always ask me. I always say yes." She paused a moment and added, "I get overtime pay practically every week."

I thought, "She has a racket going here!" As she handed my paperwork to me, I felt my air conditioning rushing out of my window into the broiling Texas heat. I offered, "I guess you'll be glad when they get a guardhouse built."

Her beautiful smile kicked up a few degrees and she leaned forward; in fact, she leaned so far forward she stuck her head in my window. She said, "Mister, I hope they never build one." And then instantly her smile disappeared, signaling she meant business when she said, "And when you fill out your customer evaluation, don't you recommend they build one, either."

She had an attitude of gratitude. She took a situation that most people would find intolerable, but instead of grumbling or quitting, she turned a lemon of a job into lemonade. That's an attitude of gratitude.

When you say "Thank you" forty times a day, it cultivates your optimistic perspective. You complain less and channel your energy into making things work, which is ultimately more satisfying. I recently read a story about a woman who, after sixteen years of being home raising her kids, went on job interviews. Potential employers were less than enthusiastic about her and kept her waiting. At first she was frustrated, wasting so many hours waiting, but during that time she realized other people also got frustrated waiting and that some were willing to pay so they didn't have to wait. Inspired by that thought, she started a waiting business. Now she sends her employees out to wait in people's homes for the gas company, furniture deliveries, cable TV installers, and others who are less than punctual. Her employees are housewives too.

To my way of thinking, a person is not a success unless he is happy. Happy people are successful people. They have a thankful attitude. There is much to be thankful for and to be happy about right now.

Choose to enjoy life and reflect that by finding at least forty things a day to feel thankful for.

Try 50 new things every month. Doesn't that sound obnoxious? Put it in perspective: that's fewer than two a day. And keep them simple. For example, here is something my wife, two kids, and I do every single time one of us goes to the grocery: We buy one item we have never bought before. It's fun, adventuresome, and it introduces us to new things we might have missed out on. Here are some other ideas: Go to work by a different route if you can, and let your brain cells get fired up playing with different visuals. Look up to the tops of buildings and trees; most Americans do not look any higher than their eyebrows. Add some adventure to lunch and choose something to eat that you have never had before. Stretch your creativity by writing your "to do" list in green ink and marking off completions in purple. Embrace the unexpected by browsing in the little hole-in-the-wall stores you never go into. Change your perspective on what life is all about by volunteering your next four Saturdays to work in a homeless shelter (and take your children with you).

Why bother? Doing fifty new things a month will help you get in and stay comfortable with the rhythm of change. We are living in hyper-changing times and those who not only survive but also thrive are the ones who have gotten comfortable (not defensive) living with change. To make this your smartest year yet, let go of some comfortable habits because they hold you back. For example, instead of reading the newspaper first thing in the morning, grab a "how to" book in your hobby interest and read for ten minutes. Instead of waiting until you are in the mood to start a major project, tell yourself that you will block out thirty minutes today to get a portion of it going. Instead of leaving your job at the end of the day with a disheartening feeling of "Enough! I'll just deal with this stuff again tomorrow," use your last fifteen minutes to plan and prioritize your next day. Instead of leaving the game early so you can beat the traffic, stay and enjoy every moment and then have fun observing the world around you — so it takes an extra twenty minutes to get home. So what? Refuse to waste your energy on feeling aggravated.

Here's another reason to embrace change in a personal and continual way. Even if you were not in a confirmed journey to find greater success in your life, you would have to make big changes anyhow. Why? The Information Age is upon us.

At the start of the 21st century, the Information Age is actually a sweeping, world-wide revolution that is shaking up people's careers, as evidenced by how our jobs keep changing. Around us, we see corporate mergers, downsizing, restructuring, government and even military functions that are now out-sourced to private industry, and new growth industries that explode into our lives like rambunctious, adolescent volcanoes. Your work has probably changed significantly. Many people tell me the jobs they are doing did not exist five years ago. Others laugh and say their jobs have evolved so much in just the last few months that they are nothing like the work they initially got hired to do.

To put these changes in perspective, consider this. The last big worldwide movement was the Industrial Age. It lasted approximately two hundred years. We are at the start of the Information Age. There is nothing on the horizon to foretell its slowing down, much less its end. Likely, we will live the remainder of our lives at the start of the Information Age. But you and I have people around us who think they are going to wait this thing out! They hunker down to keep things as they are. They are choosing not to participate in the changes. Say a prayer for them because they are as doomed as dinosaurs. The world is moving at an accelerating clip and has waning patience for people who choose not to keep up. The ones who will survive and thrive in our new environment are the ones who embrace change in a personal way. One method is to try fifty new things a month so that you are personally comfortable with the rhythm of change.

Do not forget to keep your relationships fresh, as well. While speaking at a management retreat in Brattleboro, Vermont, I instructed the executive audience in the value of using this 10-20-30-40-50 Resiliency System to be the leaders that others would want to follow. At the conclusion, a young man came up to me and said, "Thank you!"

His energy was contagious so I beamed and said, "You're welcome! Thanks for what?"

"You just gave me my wife's birthday present," he exclaimed, "and I'm so excited right now I can't stand it!"

"Birthday present? What do you mean?" I asked.

"Tomorrow is her birthday," he explained. "We have been married for four years. We don't have a lot of money and I love her so much. I wanted this to be a special birthday. I didn't know what I was going to do, until you said, 'Try fifty new things a month.' That gave me an idea. Tomorrow, when she opens her card, I'm going to have written in it, 'I love you so much that every day for the next thirty days I'm going to dream up a fresh new way to tell you how much I love you.'"

Ahhhh. Isn't that romantic? What a nice guy. I suspect that most of the readers of this book would rather get a birthday gift like that than something off the shelf.

Let me ask you. Do you have somebody in your life you love more than anything in the world? What are you doing about it? You know, we could stop cars on the street and ask people how they show their love. Everyone would have a trunkload of intentions. That makes the market value for intentions exactly zero. What are you doing about it? I commend to you, for the next thirty days, dream up one fresh new way every day to say, "I love you." Watch what happens to the quality of the relationship. What happens to the quality of your RF. Best of all, watch what happens to the quality of your life! Denis Waitley says we become the people around us. But guess who the people around you are busy becoming? You! Be someone worth becoming. How to do that? There are lots of ways to become stronger, better, high-energy people. One method is this 10-20-30-40-50 Resiliency System.

To keep your supply of RF abundant, make two copies of the following formula. Tape one onto your mirror at home and the other to the side of your monitor at work.

As my friend Mike says, "If you don't ask, you don't get." As you reach for the stars, one question to ask yourself is, "Do I have enough rocket fuel?" You know the answer is yes if you use the tools for generating your supply. Let this 10-20-30-40-50 Resiliency System serve as a renewable resource for your personal energy. Have fun on your journey. And to make your trip even more satisfying, be sure to take other people to the stars with you!

10-20-30-40-50 Resiliency System

- For 10 minutes each morning I'll read something inspirational, motivational, or instructional to raise my energy and launch my day with an optimistic perspective.
- I'll spend 20 minutes a day around positive, upbeat, optimistic people. I delight in their electricity, and I become the people around me.
- I'll say 30 positive things about myself to myself daily to affirm the best in me. I become what I think about.
- I'll say "thank you" 40 times a day. I choose to enjoy life with an attitude of gratitude. Life is good — right now!
- I'll try at least 50 new things a month — which is less than two a day! Embracing change daily builds my career, dissolves anxiety, and increases fun!

About Doug Smart, CSP

Doug Smart, CSP, is a successful business owner and a former top salesperson who is authoritative and authentic. He is a consultant, keynoter, trainer, and radio show host who has spoken at over 1,000 conventions, conferences, seminars, sales rallies and management retreats. Doug is the author or co-author Magnetic Leadership, How Real People Really Get Things Done at Work, *and* Fantastic Customer Service Inside & Out. *In 1998 the National Speakers Association awarded him the prestigious Certified Speaking Professional designation, their highest certification. Contact Doug's office for an information kit on bringing The Get Smart Series to your organization.*

Contact information:
Doug Smart, CSP
Smart Business, Inc.
P.O. Box 768024
Roswell, GA 30076
Phone: (770) 587-9784
E-mail: Doug@DougSmart.com
Website: www.DougSmart.com

Stress Hardiness or Stressed-Out: You Do Have a Choice

by Jamie Montelongo

I can specifically recall a conversation my husband and I had three years ago about how much we had going on in our lives. At the time, we had two children at home, we each had our own businesses, and we were individually involved in several hours of volunteer activity each week. Also, I shared with my father the caregiving responsibilities for my mother who has Alzheimer's Disease. Life was very full indeed. We seemed to be in constant motion. The conclusion of our conversation was this: since working harder and longer was not an option, it was time to work smarter.

The stresses in my life are not unique. In fact, they are similar to many other people's, possibly yours too. Making the choice to work smarter not harder was an important turning point for me. My life is still very full with many demands. I still have my own business, which I am currently expanding. I have one son still living at home and the other in college 2,000 miles away. I am still blessed to have both my parents with me. And I believe that there are great rewards in contributing as much time as possible to worthy volunteer activities. Storm-like stressors may come your way, but the good news is that you can make the choice to become "stress hardy." You do not have to let stress rob you of your productivity, creativity, or joy. You can have the rewards that come from working smarter, not harder.

Making the Choice to Become Stress Hardy

The term "stress" is a relatively new word. I have read that the word was first coined and studied in 1936 by researcher Hans Selye. I am sure that stress was felt before that — probably since the beginning of time! I have read many articles and books that say that one of the keys to becoming stress hardy is to think in an optimistic way. So let's give it a try.

What is the upside to stress? One thing might be that when we are under stress we get a surge of adrenaline and other hormones that can give us a tremendous burst of energy. That really comes in handy when we are running for a bus, trying to hit a homerun, or grabbing for the last cashmere sweater at an end-of-season department store sale.

But like a favorite cousin who comes for a weekend visit but brings eight large suitcases, stress becomes a problem when it stays longer than necessary. Sure, when we need to surge into our passing gear, stress causes a physical reaction that gives us a boost and supercharges us to take action. That is often referred to as the "fight or flight" response.

One time my family and I flew to New York from Houston. We weren't stressed about our trip because we were looking forward to my brother-in-law's wedding. Not only was he marrying someone who would become one of my dearest friends, but it was an out-of-state wedding, so we didn't have to do anything but pack a nice change of clothes and show up. We were packed and ready to go, and even ahead of schedule! Since we were early for our flight, we decided to stop at a diner for a bite to eat. It seemed logical at the time, so that is what we did.

While we were sipping our tea in a back booth, we heard a loud voice at the front of the diner. I stood up just to get a peek of what was going on, and, to my surprise, I saw a man with a large gun, his shirt wrapped around his head with only his eyes visible, standing at the register yelling for all the money. He nervously and in a threatening voice said to someone to his left, "Hey you, hang up that phone!," and proceeded to shoot his gun.

Speaking of shooting, that is exactly what my level of stress did . . . it shot through the roof! Immediately, I pulled my three-year-old son down on the seat of the booth and covered him by lying over him. I asked him to be very quiet. My brother-in-law did the same with his two-year-old. My husband became quiet and super-alert, ready to take action if necessary. When the robber ran with his bag of money, my husband sprang into action. He made sure that the employees and customers were all right. He was the one who gave the directive to the stunned restaurant employees to call the police and lock the front door for safety's sake. The immediate stress we felt helped us to evaluate the situation and take safety measures. No one was hurt in this incident, but for a long time thinking about it made my stress level climb. I felt real stress when recounting the incident.

In spite of all this, we made it to the airport in plenty of time. But I noticed that my attitude had changed. I looked at people with suspicion. On previous visits to New York I had been impressed with the fact that New Yorkers were much friendlier than I had heard. Yes, on the previous trips I had concluded that New York was a great place, with friendly people who walked fast and talked a little funny, but who, all-in-all, were swell.

This trip for the wedding was different. Walking down a New York street, I felt threatened and a little fearful. I kept an extremely close eye on my son, even closer than usual. So what made this trip to New York very different from my visits before? Did I meet pleasant, helpful New Yorkers? Yes, I did. But my perception and focus had changed. Because of the recent diner robbery, I was concentrating on what might go wrong and what might present a danger to my family.

As with almost everything, there are upsides and downsides to stress. (Stressed spelled backwards is desserts!) The trick is to get stress to work for us, not against us. The real danger to our health comes when we allow ourselves to become chronically stressed. The major diseases common to our culture, such as heart disease, high blood pressure, and cancer, are all stress-related illnesses.

We need to remember that stress is caused, not so much by situations but by our own perceptions. Take, for example, my visits to New York City. Both times I met really wonderful people. Both times I met some not-so-polite people. I had both positive and negative experiences each time I visited. What changed was my attitude and perception. If what we think can cause more stress, then the opposite is also true! The good news is that we can change and improve our perceptions, thoughts, and beliefs. Think about it . . . the really great news is that we can control our levels of stress.

Any workman needs the right tools to get a job done. If you were going to hang a picture on the wall you would need specific tools. There are some simple and very effective tools that we should add to our inventory so that we effectively accomplish the rewarding job of becoming "stress-hardy."

Tool # 1: Positive Self-Talk

Whether you are Chatty Cathy or the Strong Silent type, the odds are that the person with whom you do the most talking and communicating with is yourself. How do you address yourself? Are you polite, kind, and forgiving? Or are you harsh, overly critical, and demanding? Has anyone ever asked you, "What are you smiling about?" Whether you choose to share that bit of self-talk or not, we all know that what we say to ourselves can cause our lips to turn up and our eyes to sparkle, or can bring our emotions and mood crashing down.

Emotions manipulate our immune system by the chemicals and hormones we produce. If you often think negatively, then the hormones cortisol and adrenaline (just to name a couple) may suppress the healthy function of the immune system. Deeply rooted negative emotions can affect our health and well being. Some people get into a habit of constantly looking at the downside. This has been called "awfulizing." Sometimes we play the "What if?" movie in our heads, and often we focus on the many things that might go wrong. Remember it is our movie! We get to write the script. If you paid to see a movie that you thought was awful, would you get up, walk out, and then ask for your money back? I hope you would. That is what I am asking you to do with your own mental movie. If you don't like the story line, then by all means get up, walk out, and change theatres.

At times we act and react in a way that is governed by long-term perceptions and beliefs that have outlived their usefulness. One time I had some friends over for dinner, including a man named Cy. I didn't know it when I planned the menu, but he absolutely hates squash of any kind, prepared in any way. I had cooked spaghetti squash in a unique recipe, which he ate and asked for seconds, and then ate that and proceeded to compliment the great meal. After learning he had eaten squash, Cy turned a shade of ghastly green and proceeded to become quite sick to his stomach. What made my dear friend so sick (as well as cautious about eating my cooking)?

I suspect that if he had not learned that he had eaten two generous helpings of squash, he would have been fine. He really believed that he hated squash, probably since he was a small child. He was truly, physically sick once he realized what he had ingested. Was it my cooking? I don't believe that for a moment! (Plus, no one else got sick.) Was it the taste? No, when someone takes a generous second helping he isn't faking, but really likes the taste of the food. So what made him turn and run for the hall bathroom? It was his belief that he hated squash and that eating it made him sick. Our perceptions and beliefs are really very powerful. Why not choose beliefs that give us the option of being stress hardy and happy? We need to sniff out the beliefs that may be deeply rooted, long-standing perceptions that still affect our actions, but have long ago outlived their usefulness.

Here are some helpful steps to vanquish negative, archaic thoughts and replace them with positive ones:

Identify negative perceptions

What are you saying to yourself? It is for certain that people who are often depressed have a lot of negative self-talk. Really listen to your self-talk. It may help to keep a journal of what it is that you are saying. When you are feeling stress build and/or you start feeling depressed, take notes. Once identified . . .

Replace the negative with positive self-talk

Don't argue with yourself. Just delete the negative, and replace it with a realistic and positive thought. Rather than beating yourself up about what went wrong, learn from the experience. Analyze what occurred, and immediately make plans to put this new knowledge to work to improve the situation.

For example, I have to admit that when my friend became ill after eating a meal I prepared, I had to fight the urge to take it personally. My first impression was to be embarrassed that after eating my food, one of my guests turned green and became ill. My first impression was to feel bad and say to myself, "Self, regardless of how nutritious and low in fat it is, you should not have made squash!" At that point I could have concluded that I would never buy or prepare squash again. But that was the moment to analyze. When I did, I realized that all my other guests liked the meal. No one else got sick. Even Cy was bragging before he started gagging.

We often tend to take situations personally when there is a bigger picture we need to see. The issue was not about my cooking, but about Cy's belief. He too had a choice. After eating a meal that he found to be very pleasing, and then learning that he had eaten squash, he too had some options. One was to react just as he did. (That reaction does seem inappropriate at a dinner party, if you ask me.) Or he could have reasoned that his meal (1) tasted good, (2) was squash, and (3) that he must have been unfair in his long-standing vegetable evaluations. Maybe he could give squash another chance. Who knows: He might have found out that zucchini squash, summer squash, acorn squash, as well as spaghetti squash, are pleasant and desirable! (As well as nutritious and low in fat.) We really do have options here!

We can't always control what happens, but we can control our perceptions and attitudes. Our attitude is more important in determining how we handle stress, and even if we feel stress at all, than what is the cause of the perceived stress. Read that again. I really want you to remember this point.

Tool #2: Laughter

The more laughter and humor you have in your life, the less room you will have for stress. Physically, some amazing things happen when we laugh. Hardy laughter has been called "internal jogging." It really is exercise for our insides. Muscles tighten and then relax. Breathing becomes deeper, helping get oxygen into our bodies and helping us to feel better. Blood circulation increases, and our digestive system improves. The body produces endorphins that help us feel and heal better.

Laughter and humor can go a long way in diffusing a stressful situation. Take, for example, our friend Tracy. Tracy is a fun-loving, big-laugh person who also happens to be weak in the department of "organization." Because of this she has a reputation for running behind schedule most of the time. We have been known to invite our friends to join us for dinner or a movie at 7:00 p.m., but Tracy gets her own special invitation for at least a half-hour earlier. While we make allowances for

Tracy because she is so much fun, her boss is not nearly as flexible. Not long ago, Tracy received a warning, then a reprimand for being 5 to 15 minutes late. Finally, she got an ultimatum that if she was late to work just once more, she would be fired. Tracy made extra effort for a week to get to work on time, even arriving early on a couple of occasions. We were all very proud of her, but knew it was just a matter of time before another tardy occurred. We had a severe south Texas rainstorm one night, which caused a power failure, and Tracy's alarm clock failed her. She awoke late, and showed up at work a good 20 minutes behind schedule.

As she walked through the front door of her office, the tension could be felt, as well as seen on the faces of her co-workers. They all knew what was coming. She was out of a job! Aware of her late arrival, her boss walked into the front office with a scowl on his face, completely ready to make good on his threat. Before he could say a word, Tracy spoke up. "Good morning Mr. Hamby. Is it true that the early bird gets the worm? I hear that there is job opening here and I just know that I can handle the work. Well, do I get the job?" Mr. Hamby's scowl didn't much change, but he did turn around, walk back to his office and close his door, without asking Tracy to collect her personal items and leave. Her quick wit and ability to use humor did wonders in diffusing a very stressful situation.

It may help to practice "Joy Jotting." Why not take a couple of minutes at the end of your day to jot down some of the good things that have happened. Smile about them, and go to sleep thinking of the blessings in your life. Remember even the situations that do not go as we hope are valuable opportunities for us to learn, grow, become more empathetic, and do better the next time.

Tool #3: Love and companionship

There was a story recounted at a business seminar dealing with human relationships. The speaker told of a home for orphaned children. Inside this home was a long row where the babies were kept in their cribs. Some of these babies became ill and some of them died . . . except the baby in the last crib. This baby did better than expected. The doctor was perplexed. The care provided was consistent, since all were fed, bathed, and kept warm. Yet only the baby in the last crib thrived. As months passed and new babies were brought in, the story remained the same: Only the baby in the last crib did well. The doctor concealed himself to observe, so that he might find an explanation for the one child's robust condition.

At midnight the cleaning woman came in, and, on hands and knees, scrubbed the floor, from one end to the other. After finishing her scrubbing, she stood up, stretched, and rubbed her back. Then she went to the last crib, picked up the baby, walked around the room with him, cuddling him, talking to him, rocking him in her arms. She put him back in the crib and left. The doctor watched night after night, and each night the same thing happened. It was always the baby in the last crib who got picked up, cuddled, talked to, and loved. And in all the new groups of babies brought in, it was always the baby in the last crib who thrived, while the others got sick and some died.

Psychology Today reported that "during formative periods of brain growth, certain kinds of sensory deprivation . . . such as a lack of touching and rocking by the mother . . . result in incomplete or damaged development of the neuronal systems that control affection."

Loving, caring human relationships are vital to our health. Thus the opposite, the lack of companionship, can be detrimental. We are faced with many pressures in modern living, such as broken homes, single-parent families, emotionally neglected children, preoccupation with material things, the collapse of morals, and the loss of true values . . . all of which add to the instability and loneliness that damage our health and increase our stress.

Many clinical studies support that there are medical consequences of loneliness. Humans have biological needs for love and human companionship, and the failure to meet these needs may be ultimately exacted within our own hearts and blood vessels. So what do you do if you find yourself feeling lonely? It is true that one may not have the love, support, and companionship biologically necessary for happiness, health and stress-hardiness within the established relationships with our parents, our mates or our children, but it is up to us to go out and create the relationships we need.

Look to see what you can do within your own block, your own street, your own building. There are always children who can benefit from our concern. Always a lonely person hoping for a friendship ready to be cultivated. Always a lonely older person whose family lives far away, who could use a friendly visit or help.

The point is that love (and companionship) is essential to humans. When we have it in abundance, our stress is reduced. An example of this occurred in the town of Roseto, Pennsylvania. There was a very low death rate from coronary heart disease. The epidemiologists studying the inhabitants of Roseto expected to find a community of physically active, non-smoking, nutritionally conscious individuals. They got a big surprise! The people in Roseto had basically terrible health habits and were found to be high in the risk factors for heart disease. But they did have a major protective factor in their favor: the social environment of the community. There was a large extended family atmosphere there. People tended to grow up there, and stay there to begin their own lives. There was a great deal of support and connection. Within the community, when a problem arose, people were available to help out, listen, and show concern. The study also showed that when people moved out of

Roseto, their rate of heart attack rose to the predicted level. Connection, love, and social support proved to be more important than health habits in predicting heart disease.

As mentioned before, we need to sniff out the beliefs that may be deeply rooted, long-standing perceptions that still effect our actions, but have long ago outlived their usefulness. So how can we overcome conditioning that causes us to close down in fear rather than be open to feelings of love, connection, and trust? Again we need to (1) identify our negative thoughts and (2) replace them with positive self-talk. One very effective way to counter stress is to cultivate an attitude of openness to love and forgiveness, both to ourselves and to others.

Tool #4: Before there was Prozac there was Massage

In a society of "instant everything" we all seem to be running at warp speed. Then the inevitable happens: Our bodies get sick in order to slow us down. Our bodies are wonderful and will heal and serve us well if we make it our priority to take control and make sure that we have the time, space, and environment we need to heal and counter the negative effects of stress. One of the oldest, safest and most valuable therapies is Touch Therapy, or therapeutic massage.

Every living creature has a craving and a biological need to be touched. Touch is as important as food and water. Massage therapy acts as the perfect antidote for stress, while fulfilling our need for touch. Massage sends a message to the body to slow down and relax. With this relaxation comes a harmony, a sense of wholeness and peace. It helps us listen to and understand the messages that our body is sending us. Once we "hear our bodies" messages, we can respond by making needed changes to get rid of that headache, slow down, create some alone time, or just make it a point to breathe deeply and get needed rest.

When we care enough for our bodies to spend the time and money to take care of them, it sends a message to our subconscious that we have value and significance. How can others treat us with respect, if we don't respect ourselves? Get a massage. You deserve it! Besides, this is the only body you are going to get. You will do well to take care of it.

Ask people you know if they can recommend a good massage therapist. Visit several, and then choose one with whom you feel comfortable. Or, contact The International Massage Association (IMA) or the American Massage Therapy Association (AMTA) for therapists working in your area.

Many companies are offering regular massage as an employee benefit. Seated-massage, onsite at the workplace, is an effective and low-cost way of helping employees deal with job-related stress. Some of the benefits are listed below.

Massage does the following:

- Reduces the physical and mental effects of stress and thus helps prevent burnout and stress-related illnesses
- Relieves the adverse effects of sitting for long periods of time in the same position
- Relieves physical problems associated with repetitive tasks, e.g. computer work, sorting, filing, and assembly line tasks
- Improves alertness and ability to focus
- Helps relieve common problems, such as tension headaches and stiff, sore muscles
- Improves immune system functioning for better general health and resistance to colds and other illnesses
- Leaves one feeling revitalized and ready to return to work

Tool #5: Apply Ergonomic Principles to Work Smarter, not Harder

Navigating through your stress-filled life is a lot like flying a plane through a storm. Over a hundred instruments fill the panels on the flight deck of a large airplane. A skilled pilot will rely on the information conveyed from takeoff to landing, and will use this information to make wise decisions. Like the essential instrumentation on a plane, your body communicates vital information to you each moment of every day. From morning until night, or from take off until safe landing, you need to pay heed to the critical information conveyed. In other words, when your body speaks, please listen.

Because stress can cause greater susceptibility to physical injury, one way of working smarter is to become familiar with basic ergonomic principles that can easily be applied in daily life. A simple definition of ergonomics is the science of fitting the job to the worker. When there is a mismatch between the physical requirements of the job and the physical capacity of the worker, there is an increased risk for development of musculoskeletal disorders (MSD's).

Ergonomic Principle #1: Neutral Posture

Whether maintaining a position or making a movement, the joints should be kept in neutral posture to the extent possible. Neutral posture is the position where the joints and ligaments are stretched to the least possible extent and, therefore, are subject to less physical stress. Some examples of non-neutral postures are working with bent wrists, bent neck and turned head, raised arms, twisted and/or bent trunk.

Ergonomic Principle #2: Keep the Work Close to Your Body

With your work close, you are able to stay in neutral posture more of the time. In my massage therapy practice I have had clients with shoulder and neck pain which resulted from reaching for the phone frequently throughout their workday. By moving the phone closer, they were able to spend more time working in neutral posture, decreasing the amount of stress on shoulder muscles and joints. The most notable result was less shoulder and neck pain. There are times when a simple change can lead to a remarkable outcome.

Ergonomic Principle #3: Alternate Positions and Movements

Maintaining rigid positions or postures, and repetitive movements are taxing, and over a period of time can lead to muscle and joint injuries. The negative results of static postures and repetitive movements can be avoided by alternating tasks and taking "micro breaks." Vary the tasks that make up your day, while still accomplishing what you need to get done.

"Since stress is the nonspecific response of the body to any demand, everybody is always under some degree of stress," to quote Dr. Hans Selye once again. To say you have stress is like saying you have a body temperature.

How you respond to stress depends on many factors. Regardless of its cause, though, stress can be managed. It is my sincere desire that the five fundamental tools presented in this chapter will be used by you to make the choice to be stress hardy instead of stressed-out. Refuse to allow stress to rob you of your joy and passion for living! In other words, work smarter, not harder!

ABOUT JAMIE MONTELONGO

Jamie Montelongo is a registered massage therapist and owner of Touchstone Massage Therapy Clinic. She specializes in therapeutic massage and trigger point therapy for pain and stress relief. Her areas of expertise include pregnancy massage, pain relief therapy for people with fibromyalgia and MSD's, such as carpal tunnel and TMJ. She is a member of the International Massage Association (IMA). Jamie is certified in prenatal and peri-natal massage, and is a certified lactation educator from the University of California at Los Angeles. Jamie educates companies and organizations regarding stress relief and implementation of ergonomic principles in the workplace. Jamie lives with her family in San Antonio.

Contact Information:
Jamie Montelongo
Touchstone Massage Therapy
4118 McCullough, Suite 21
San Antonio, TX 78212
Phone: (210) 710-5512
Fax: (210) 494-3882
E-mail: Jamiermt@juno.com

RESOURCE LISTING

Valerie Bernard
Executive Training Centers, Inc.
2808 Birch Avenue
Point Pleasant, WV 25550
Phone: (304) 593-2401
E-mail: etcwv@charter.net
Website: www.etcwv.com and www.ogmandino.com/etcwv

Louis B. Cady, M.D.
611 Harriet Street, Suite 304
Doctors Plaza
Evansville, IN 47710
Phone: (812) 429-0772
Fax: (812) 429-0793
E-mail: LCady@DrCady.com
Website: www.DrCady.com

Lynn Hauser
Performance Partners, Inc.
P.O. Box 757
Frankfort, IL 60423-0757
Phone: (815) 464-5472
E-mail: lynn@performancepartnersinc.net
Website: www.lynnspeaks.com

Cynthia Mustaine Hettinger
Electra's Acres
9374 North Marzane Road
Markle, IN 46770
Phone: 260-638-0050
E-Mail: electrasacres@aol.com
Website: www.electrasacres.com

Greg Jordan
Peak Performance Solutions Inc.
Phone: (515) 554 4305
E-mail: greg@peak-ps.com
Website: www.peak-ps.com

Debra Kimbrough
P.O. Box 1539
Kemah, TX 77565
Phone: (281) 339-4507
E-mail: debra@debrakimbrough.com
Website: DebraKimbrough.com

Jamie Montelongo
Touchstone Massage Therapy
4118 McCullough, Suite 21
San Antonio, TX 78212
Phone: (210) 710-5512
Fax: (210) 494-3882
E-mail: Jamiermt@juno.com

Doug Smart, CSP
Smart Business, Inc.
P.O. Box 768024
Roswell, GA 30076
Phone: (770) 587-9784
E-mail: Doug@DougSmart.com
Website: www.DougSmart.com

Chad Terry, CSA
Financially Speaking
15053 Rosewood Drive
Clive, IA 50325
Phone: (515) 778-0292
E-mail: chad@financiallyspeaking.biz
Website: www.financiallyspeaking.biz

Michelle M. Weil, Ph.D.
Human-Ware, LLC
Phone: (760) 730-3894
E-Mail: Weil@Human-Ware.com
Website: www.Human-Ware.com